A Music Course for Students

Second edition

Geoffrey Winters
with D. E. Parry Williams

Oxford University Press
Music Department, Walton Street, Oxford OX2 6DP

major / minor scales
p.45

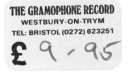

Oxford books for music examinations

CSE and O level
Music from Scratch (a music course for CSE) Tony Attwood
Shapes and Structures in Music (an introduction to musical form)
Michael Callaghan and Graham Williams

O and A level
Preparing for Examinations (Books 1 and 2) Edwin Smith and
David Renouf
Aural Analysis Celia Duffy and Roger Parker

General
Elementary Harmony (complete) C. H. Kitson
Elementary Harmony (Part 1) C. H. Kitson
The Oxford Student's Harmony Edwin Smith and David Renouf

First published 1986
Reprinted 1990, 1991
ISBN 0 19 321840 2

Printed in Great Britain by J. W. Arrowsmith Ltd., Bristol

Acknowledgements

We are grateful to the following for permission to reproduce
extracts of their copyright material:
Boosey & Hawkes Music Publishers Ltd. p 28, 181 Bartók:
Concerto for Ochestra, p 44 Britten: *Serenade* Prologue and
Elegy, p 163 Shostakovich: *Spring Quartet No. 8*; Universal
Edition (London) Ltd. p 31 Bartók: *Spring Quartet 5*, p 46
Schoenberg: *6 Kleine Klavierstücke;* Oxford University Press
p 4, p 34, p 164 Vaughan Williams: *Symphony No. 6.*

Preface

Dr Parry Williams's *A Music Course for Students* was first published in 1937, and its considerable success has continued to the present day. This must surely arise from its comprehensive coverage, its clarity of presentation, its convenient format and its relevance to the needs of teachers and students.

However, even examinations change and gradually over the years a number of requirements have slipped quietly away and in their place, others, particularly those to do with analysis and orchestral instruments, have taken their place. Anyone familiar with the original will instantly recognize how closely in my revision I have adhered to the overall chapter plan. Only Chapter V, originally Three-Part Writing, now Texture, Timbre and Transposition departs nominally from the plan, but even here, a closer look will reveal that a good deal of the content is derived from the earlier book. Specific exercises, after great consideration, have been omitted as these are now readily available in a number of forms. The space gained has allowed a slightly more expansive treatment of some areas and the inclusion of a number of complete music examples.

My aim has been, whilst keeping within the spirit of the original, to re-order and recast the material in a form which more easily allows a progression through the book, with less need to make cross-references to other chapters for elucidation on related points. Hence melody and very rudimentary harmony are treated side by side in Chapter II, rather than as separate entities as was formerly adopted. Chapter III introduces inversions and bass lines through the medium of two-part writing, so that when in Chapter IV a fuller study of harmony is introduced in the context of four-part vocal harmony, many of the basic procedures have already been encountered in easier settings. Chapter V brings together much valuable material from the original and supplements it with information on wind instruments and orchestral scores as well as with a fuller treatment of the perennial problem of transposition.

Throughout the book, but particularly in Chapter VI (Structure and Form) longer extracts have been added in the form of Annotated Examples, so that the details covered in adjacent sections can be reviewed, whilst at the same time observing some of the labelling and analytical techniques called for by many examining boards. The Chronology of Composers has been augmented with a few composers like Telemann, Vivaldi and Mahler who have become part of our daily diet in recent decades and in addition a short note about each composer has been added, hopefully, as a not too misleading guide to the student, who wishes to grasp something of

PREFACE

the place and style of that composer before delving further. With the growing importance of setting a subject more widely, the Comparative Chronology has been broadened to include political, scientific and social events, as well as to include writers from other countries. It has of course been lengthened – at both ends! It is hoped that this revision will not only fulfil the needs of the O level student as did the original, but will also prove of use to the less advanced student and to the instrumentalist and listener who wish to understand more of the internal structure of their subject.

Geoffrey Winters   1984

Contents

CONTENTS

CONTENTS

CONTENTS

CONTENTS

CONTENTS

CONTENTS

CONTENTS

CONTENTS

CONTENTS

VI Structure and form

CONTENTS

Chronology of composers and their works

CONTENTS

CONTENTS

I The Rudiments of Music

A Pulse and duration

1 Most music has an underlying pulse or beat, which can be shown by a series of equal signs, called **notes**, like this:

This note ♩ is called a **crotchet**. Each crotchet represents one beat or pulse, although, as will be explained later, the beat can be represented by notes other than crotchets.

2 Sounds which last *longer* than a crotchet are shown in the following ways:

    ♩ a minim (= 2 crotchets)

    ♩. a dotted minim (= 3 crotchets)

    o a semibreve (= 4 crotchets)

3 Sounds which last *less* than a crotchet have tails on their stems. (It does not matter here whether the stems are up or down, but look later at section C18.)

    ♪ a quaver (= ½ a crotchet)

    ♫ a pair of quavers lasts one crotchet

    ♪ a semiquaver (= ¼ of a crotchet)

    ♬ a group of four semiquavers lasts one crotchet

    ♪ a demisemiquaver (= ⅛ of a crotchet)

    ♬ a group of eight demisemiquavers lasts one crotchet

Even smaller subdivisions occur, but more rarely.

4 These shorter notes can be grouped into other patterns, or rhythms, equal to one crotchet:

5 Any note can be shown to last half as long again by adding a dot, like this:

♩.   a dotted crotchet (= 1½ crotchets)

♩.   a dotted minim (= 1½ minims, or 3 crotchets)

♪.   a dotted quaver (= 1½ quavers, or ¾ of a crotchet)

6 Silences in a piece of music are shown by **rests**. Each note has its equivalent rest.

	Note	Rest	Duration (when beat equals one crotchet)
semibreve	o	–	4 beats
minim	♩	–	2 beats
crotchet	♩	‡	1 beat
quaver	♪	⌐	½ beat
semiquaver	♪	⌐	¼ beat
demisemiquaver	♪	⌐	⅛ beat

7 Rests, like notes, may also be lengthened by dots, or the additional silence may be shown by an extra rest of half the value of the original rest, i.e.

𝄽.   or   𝄽   ⌐

B   Accent and time: bars

1 Music falls naturally into a regular pattern of stressed and unstressed beats. The position of these stressed, or **accented**, beats is shown by adding a **bar-line** in front of the accented beat.

2   The beats which occur between bar-lines make up a **bar** (or **measure**) and most commonly consist of:

     2 beats in a bar (duple time)

     3 beats in a bar (triple time)

     4 beats in a bar (quadruple time)

Examples with a greater number of beats occur, but more rarely.

3   The number of beats in a bar is shown by a **time signature**, placed at the beginning of the piece: $\frac{2}{4}$ $\frac{3}{4}$ $\frac{4}{4}$ $\frac{5}{4}$

It looks like a fraction. The upper figure gives the number of beats in a bar, and the lower figure shows which type of note represents a beat. Here the figure 4 indicates a crotchet beat. (For an explanation of this lower number, see section G.) Thus, $\frac{2}{4}$ is an example of duple time, and $\frac{3}{4}$ is an example of triple time, both with a crotchet beat.

4   The end of a piece or section is shown with a **double bar-line** (the second line is usually thicker), i.e.   ‖

5   Within this regular framework of bar-lines, any pattern of notes is possible, so long as the total number of beats within each bar remains the same.

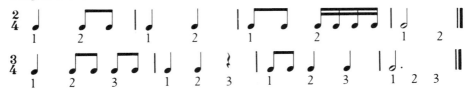

6   Ties are used to write note-values which cannot be shown in any other way.

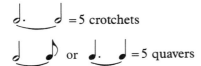

(Ties are also used to clarify the grouping of notes, particularly in the middle of bars.)

7   They are also used for sounds which extend over a bar-line into the next bar, e.g.

Here the first sound lasts four beats (3 + 1) and the last note of the third bar is joined by a tie across the bar-line to make a two-beat sound.

8 Rests are never tied.

Annotated examples for I A and B

Borodin: *Polovtsian Dances* (II)

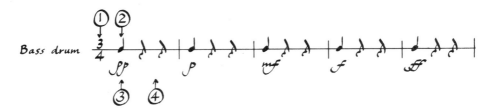

1 Time signature: three crotchet beats in a bar.
2 One crotchet.
3 Initials from Italian words for degrees of loudness – very soft to very loud (see I T4).
4 Two crotchet rests on 2nd and 3rd beats.

Tchaikovsky: *Danse russe Trepak*

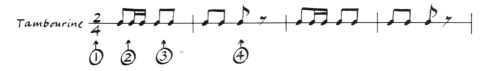

1 Time signature: two crotchet beats in a bar.
2 One quaver and two semiquavers, equalling one beat.
3 Two quavers equalling one beat.
4 Single quaver followed by quaver rest, equalling one beat.

Vaughan Williams: *Symphony No. 6* (2nd movement)

1   Time signature: four crotchet beats in a bar.
2   Two semiquavers and one quaver, equalling one beat (beat 1).
3   Quaver rest followed by two semiquavers, equalling one beat (beat 2).
4   Quaver, followed by quaver rest, equalling one beat (beat 3).
5   Two semiquavers and one quaver, equalling one beat (beat 4).

Kodály: *Háry János Suite* (4th movement)

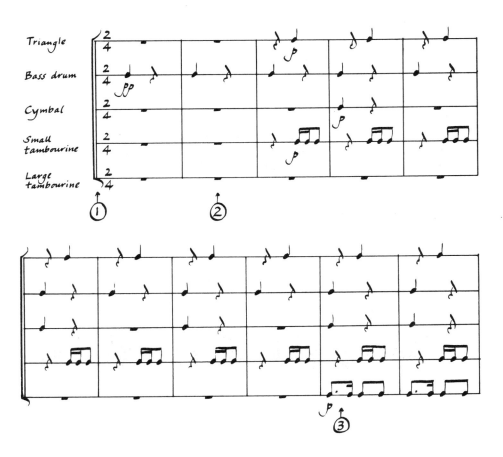

1   Conductor's score showing five percussion parts.
2   Semibreve rest used for whole bar's silence.
3   Dotted quaver (¾ beat) and semiquaver (¼ beat) equal one beat.

C Pitch

The staff, or stave

1 Percussion instruments, such as drums and tambourine, are used for rhythm, contrast, and colour. Each plays a single sound which is largely determined by its size. So it is sufficient to write their parts on a single line.

2 Melodic instruments and voices are able to vary the pitch of the sounds they make: they play and sing both high and low sounds.

3 Early attempts at notation placed notes

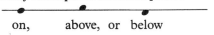

    on,   above, or below

a line, to show their relative pitch.

4 Nowadays we use a set of five parallel lines called a **staff**, or **stave**, to indicate the precise pitch of the sounds. Notes are written either on a line (with a line running through the middle) or in a space (between two lines). The pattern made by the notes forms a picture or map of the sounds to be played or sung:

5 Each individual note has a letter name
A B C D E F G
After G the alphabetical sequence is repeated, because the next note sounds the same as the first A, only at a higher pitch. The span of eight notes between two notes of the same letter name is called an **octave**.

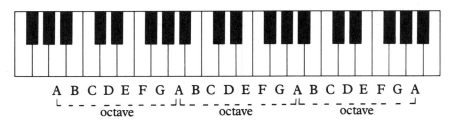

The treble clef

6 In order to notate a particular range of notes we add a **clef** at the beginning of each stave of music.

7   One of the most common clefs is the **treble clef** (or G clef) which covers the range of notes produced by the soprano voice, by relatively high-pitched instruments, or by the top half of the piano keyboard. It looks like this:

It is called the G clef because the clef sign curls round the second line up of the stave, fixing the pitch of that note as G. (On the piano keyboard this is the G five notes above the central C on the keyboard, known as Middle C.)

8   On the stave, the alphabetical sequence of notes looks like this in the treble clef:

      D   E   F   G   A   B   C   D   E   F   G

9   This sequence of adjacent notes is called a **scale**.

10   In order to continue the sequence of notes higher or lower, short **leger lines** are used to extend the stave:

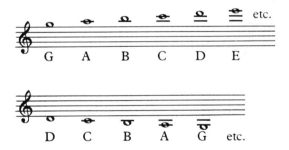

The bass clef

11   The other most commonly used clef is the **bass** or **F clef**, which covers the range of notes produced by the bass voice, by relatively low-pitched instruments, or by the bottom half of the piano keyboard. It looks like this:

The symbol is derived from the letter F, and the two dots fix the fourth line up as the F below Middle C.

12 On the stave, the alphabetical sequence of notes looks like this in the bass clef:

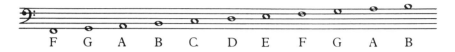

F   G   A   B   C   D   E   F   G   A   B

13 Leger lines can again be used to extend the stave:

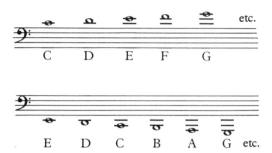

C   D   E   F   G   etc.

E   D   C   B   A   G   etc.

14 Now Middle C is on a leger line above the bass stave, and like other notes in the mid-range it can be written in two ways, either below the treble stave, or above the bass:

Middle C   Middle C

15 Pianists play with both hands so two staves are coupled together with a **brace**. The upper stave for the *right* hand usually has a treble clef, the lower stave for the *left* hand, a bass clef. However, occasionally the right hand may play a passage in the bass clef or the left hand in the treble, in which case two bass or two treble clefs are used:

16 Here is the bass-treble range of the notes so far studied and their relationship to the keyboard:

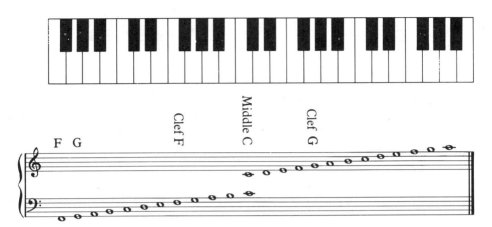

17 Mnemonics are of help in memorizing the names of the lines and spaces of the two clefs.

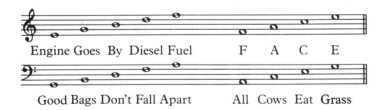

Engine Goes By Diesel Fuel   F   A   C   E

Good Bags Don't Fall Apart   All Cows Eat Grass

18 Note stems *above* the middle line are usually written *downwards* to the left of the notehead:

and those *below* the middle line *upwards*, with the stem to the right of the note-head:

9

Notes on the middle line may have their stems placed either way according to context:

or

Where two parts are written on one stave, the upper part has all its stems upward and the lower one downward, even where the parts cross over as at *x*. Where both parts sing or play the same sound, upward and downward stems are attached to the same notehead. In the case of a semibreve, the note is duplicated and interlocked.

Annotated examples for I C

Beethoven: *Symphony No. 1* (4th movement)

Violin I

1   Treble clef, fixing second line up as G.
2   Incomplete bar starting with a semiquaver rest.
3   Scale passage from G to upper G.
4   Dots above or below a note shorten the note and detach it from the next (*staccato*).
5   Slur between different notes indicates method of bowing on violin (see V F).

Sweelinck: Variations on *Est-ce Mars* (No. 1)

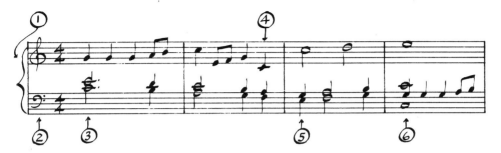

1 Brace joins two staves.
2 Bass clef, with two dots fixing fourth line up as F.
3 Middle C on leger line above bass stave, with the E above it on a second leger line.
4 Middle C on leger line below treble stave.
5 Upward and downward stems indicate two distinct parts.
6 Tune from bar 1 returns an octave lower in tenor part.

The C clef

19 Although most music is written in either the treble or the bass clef, a third clef is sometimes used to notate music which lies awkwardly in the range around Middle C. It is called the **C clef**, and it looks like this:

Like the other two clefs, it derives its shape from the relevant letter (C) and it fixes the line running through the middle of the clef (the middle line of the stave in the example above) as Middle C.

20 Unlike the treble and bass clefs, which nowadays are fixed, the C clef has always been movable. When used on the middle line, it is known as the **alto clef**, and when used on the fourth line, as the **tenor clef**. Some editions of early vocal music are still found with their original C clefs on the other three lines: **baritone** on the top line, **mezzo soprano** on the second line (making it Middle C, not G, as with the treble clef), and on the lowest line the **soprano** clef.

Alto	Tenor	Mezzo-Soprano	Soprano	Baritone
Middle C	Middle C	Middle C	Middle C	Middle C

21 The alto clef is (with the exception of vocal music) used exclusively for viola music.

22 The tenor clef is also found in vocal scores, and is used for higher passages in music for cello and bassoon, and for the tenor trombone.

23 When working with C clefs, calculate the notes upwards and downwards, alternate lines and spaces, from the line marked as Middle C. Although at first confusing, C clefs can save the use of unnecessary leger lines for singers and instrumentalists whose range lies in a middle pitch register.

Viola

written in the treble clef becomes:

and in the bass clef:

D Tones and semitones

1 Compare the alphabetical sequence of notes with the keyboard diagram.

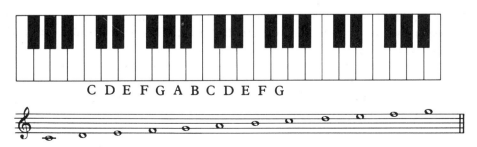

C D E F G A B C D E F G

2 Notice that some steps, like C to D and D to E, are separated by a black note. These are **whole tones** or **tones**.

3 Others like E to F and B to C have no black note between, are closer in sound and are **half tones** or **semitones**.

4 Tones and semitones can be played on other instruments, e.g. on a guitar, semitones are one fret apart, tones are two frets.

5 On a keyboard, tones also occur between a white and black note and between two black notes, in which case they are separated by a white note. Semitones occur between adjacent white and black notes.

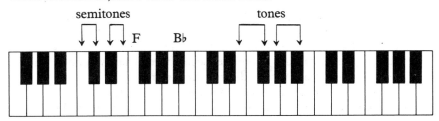

6 A tone is equal to two semitones.

7 A black note which sounds a semitone higher than its nearest white note is notated by adding a sharp ♯ in front of the written note, e.g. F♯ is just to the right of F and is written:

8 A black note which sounds a semitone lower than its nearest white note is notated by adding a flat ♭ in front of the written note, e.g. B♭ is just to the left of B and is written:

9 Any note may be changed in a similar way.

E Accidentals

1 As we have seen in the previous section:
a sharp ♯ raises a note by a semitone,
a flat ♭ lowers a note by a semitone.

These signs are known as **accidentals**. Sometimes we need to cancel a sharp or a flat in order to restore the note to its original state. In this case a natural sign ♮ is used, which raises a flattened note, or lowers a sharpened note by a semitone.

More rarely:

a **double sharp** x raises a sharp note an additional semitone,
a **double flat** ♭♭ lowers a flat note an additional semitone.

2   Remember to write the accidental in front of the note and notice, for example, that we say 'F sharp' but we write 'sharp F' so that the performer is warned of the change before he makes the sound.

3   An accidental normally applies only to the notes in the bar in which it occurs. Sometimes a cautionary accidental (often in brackets) is used in a subsequent bar as a reminder that the previous accidental no longer applies.

In addition, accidentals are sometimes seen above or below a note. These are often in brackets or small print and serve three purposes:

a) to show an editorial suggestion, especially in early music.
b) to reassure a player that the sound he is to play is as written despite its conflict with a note in another part.
c) to show whether an ornamental trilling note is a semitone or a tone away from the principal note. (See I S.)

F   Scales and key signatures

1   The word **scale** is derived from the Latin **scala**, meaning 'ladder'.

2   Any ordered stepwise arrangement of sounds upwards or downwards constitutes a scale.

3   Scales follow an alphabetical sequence of notes which span an octave, before repeating themselves at a higher or lower pitch. They mostly contain seven different notes, the eighth note being the same as the first.

4   The scale which sounds most familiar to our ears is the **major scale**, which can be produced by playing the eight white notes on a keyboard instrument, from C to C.

5   That this sounds 'right' or 'normal' is due to the particular arrangement of intervals within the octave. As we saw in D3, the intervals E – F and B – C are both semitones.

6 The remaining intervals are all **whole tones** (equal to two semitones)

C major

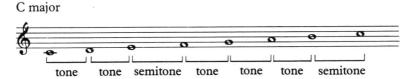

| tone | tone | semitone | tone | tone | tone | semitone |

7 The first (or last) note of the scale is called the **keynote**, and it gives its name to the scale. In Tonic Sol-fa it is called 'doh'.

8 Its technical name is the **tonic**. Each degree of the scale is named according to its numerical position and relationship to the tonic.

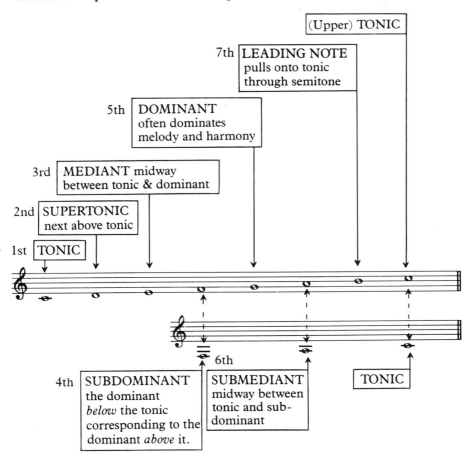

(Upper) TONIC

7th LEADING NOTE
pulls onto tonic
through semitone

5th DOMINANT
often dominates
melody and harmony

3rd MEDIANT midway
between tonic & dominant

2nd SUPERTONIC
next above tonic

1st TONIC

4th SUBDOMINANT
the dominant
below the tonic
corresponding to the
dominant *above* it.

6th SUBMEDIANT
midway between
tonic and sub-
dominant

TONIC

9   The **major scale** is formed from two four-note groups called **tetrachords**. Each tetrachord has an identical arrangement of two tones and a semitone. The **lower tetrachord** starts on the tonic, and the **upper tetrachord** on the dominant.

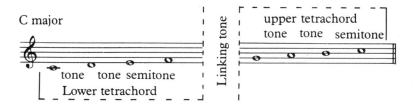

10 By playing or singing the upper tetrachord first,

and then adding another (white note) tetrachord above this:

we form a new scale:

11 Notice that the new tetrachord is not the same in its arrangement of tones and semitones. In particular the seventh note is too low and does not lead to the tonic. To preserve the major scale pattern, this seventh note is raised by means of a sharp (see E above). This correction changes the position of the semitone in the upper tetrachord and makes the pattern the same as that of the lower.

Now the scale sounds like a major scale. It takes its name from its new keynote or tonic, which is G. So every piece of music written in the key of G major requires a sharp in front of every F.

12 To avoid the unnecessary use of accidentals in major keys other than C, we extract any sharps (or flats) to a position at the beginning of each line, immediately after the clef.

13 Such groups of sharps (or flats) are arranged in a fixed pattern and enable the performer to identify the scale or key of the music. They are called **key signatures**. No key signature is required for C major, and those for the other keys have up to seven sharps or flats, but never a mixture of both.

14 So we can write the scale of G major as follows:

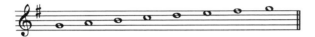

Although the sharp sign in the key signature always occurs on the same line, it indicates that *all* Fs, whatever their pitch, are to be sharpened.

15 Major scales can be formed successively by superimposing new upper tetrachords. Each new scale starts on the fifth note of the preceding scale, and each additional sharp is moved to the new key signature. All existing sharps are retained, and the newly-added sharp is always the seventh note of the new key.

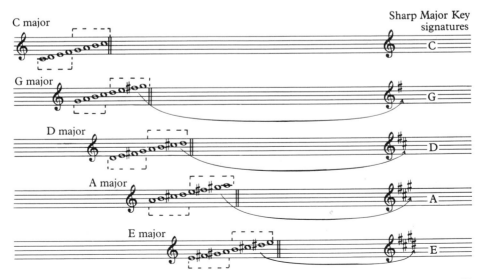

B major

F# major

16 In addition to major scales with sharp key signatures, there is a corresponding series, or **cycle**, with flats, beginning with the scale of F major. It can be formed by taking the lower tetrachord of C major and using this as the **upper** tetrachord of the new scale.

Below this, add a new tetrachord with identical intervals starting on a flattened B:

Now add the accidental B flat to the key signature:

The series continues as below. Each new scale starts on the fourth note of the preceding scale. Each additional flat is moved to the key signature. All existing flats are retained, and the newly-added flat is always on the fourth note.

F major

Flat Major Key signatures

Bb major

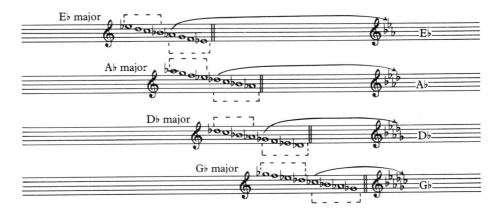

17 The cycle of major key signatures in both treble and bass clefs is shown below. Each new key starts on the dominant (or fifth note) of the previous key. There are only twelve distinct major scales, corresponding to the twelve notes within an octave, but some can be written in two ways, e.g. F sharp major and G flat minor, which sound exactly the same.

E

A

D

G

C

Annotated examples for I D, E and F

Handel: *Courante*

1   Key signature of F major, one flat on middle line.
2   B flat in bass clef comes on second line.
3   Descending scale of F major.
4   Ascending scale of F major in Bass.
5   Accidental B natural raises B flat by semitone.
6   In the following three bars, all B flats are cancelled with naturals. The passage has changed key, or **modulated** (see I Q) to C major, which is the dominant of F major.
7   Ascending scale of C major, with B natural as leading note.

Liszt: *Hungarian Rhapsody No. 2*

1   Treble clef on lower stave and bass clef on upper, showing crossed-hands position on piano keyboard.
2   Key signature of six sharps indicates F sharp major.
3   Staccato dots indicate detached articulation.
4   F double sharp (×) leading to G sharp.
5   Crushed notes, or **acciaccaturas**, each 'crushed' onto a note one semitone higher (see I S).
6   Treble clef restored for right hand.

Debussy: *La fille aux cheveux de lin* (Préludes, Book 1)

1   Key signature of six flats indicates G flat major.
2   Instructions for tempo and mood in French, characteristic of Debussy (see I T 6).
3   Crotchet tied to quaver, equivalent to ♩. as used in bar 5.
4   Short scale passage, see extension at end of extract.
5   Chord tied across bar-line.
6   First phrase repeated with left hand accompaniment. Accidental F flat eventually leads down to E flat at end of next bar.
7   C flat restores key signature after C naturals.
8   Considerable extension of scale passage with some notes tied over to create a chord.

G   Simple and compound times and time signatures

1   $\frac{2}{4}$, $\frac{3}{4}$ and $\frac{4}{4}$ are all examples of **simple** time. In all simple times the beat divides naturally into multiples of two.

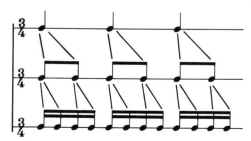

2   Quite often, the beat divides into multiples of *three* rather than two, in which case the time is known as **compound**. The most commonly-found example of compound time is ⁶₈, where two dotted crotchet beats (♩.) are each divisible into three quavers (♫♪) or unequally into a crotchet and a quaver (♩ ♪):

Vln   Haydn: *Symphony No. 101* (1st movement)

3   As there are two dotted crotchet beats, ⁶₈ is an example of duple time. It is, however, unrelated to ³₄ time despite also having six quavers in a bar. The grouping of notes into twos or threes distinguishes one from the other.

Notice also that the whole bar in each time is filled with a dotted minim. In ⁶₈ time this is equal to two dotted crotchets, but in ³₄ to three crotchets.

        i.e. 2 beats   ⁶₈ 𝅗𝅥. = ♩. ♩.

        i.e. 3 beats   ³₄ 𝅗𝅥. = ♩ ♩ ♩

4   Although ⁶₈ strictly means 'six quaver beats in a bar' (8 denoting a quaver − see B 3), in practice ⁶₈ always means 'two dotted crotchet beats in a bar'.

5   Similarly, ⁹₈ indicates 'three dotted crotchet beats in a bar' (compound triple time), and ¹²₈ 'four dotted crotchet beats in a bar' (compound quadruple time).

6   Notice that the *lower* number in the time signature always equals the number of beats contained in a semibreve:

     4 indicates 'crotchet' − there are four crotchets in a semibreve
     8 indicates 'quaver' − there are eight quavers in a semibreve.

     Similarly, if the bottom number is 2, it indicates that the beat is a *minim* (there being two minims in a semibreve). And if it is 16 (rare), it indicates that the beat is a semiquaver (there being 16 semiquavers in a semibreve).

It is for this reason that, in American usage, the semibreve is called a 'whole note', the minim a 'half note', the crotchet a 'quarter note', the quaver an 'eighth note', and the semiquaver a 'sixteenth note'.

7   The main simple time signatures are shown below:

	Duple	**Triple**	**Quadruple**	**Quintuple**
¼ note or crotchet beat	2 4	3 4	4 4	5 4
½ note or minim beat	2 2	3 2	4 2 (mostly hymns)	5 2 (rare)
⅛ note or quaver beat	2 8 (rare)	3 8	4 8	5 8

8   The main compound time signatures are shown below:

	Duple	**Triple**	**Quadruple**	**Quintuple**
dotted crotchet beat expressed as three quavers	6 8	9 8	12 8	15 8
dotted minim beat expressed as three crotchets	6 4	9 4	12 4	15 4
dotted quaver beat expressed as three semiquavers	6 16	9 16	12 16	15 16

Of these, only $\frac{6}{8}$, $\frac{9}{8}$, $\frac{12}{8}$ and $\frac{6}{4}$ are commonly encountered.

With all compound time signatures, the upper figure must be divided by *three* to give the number of beats in a bar. The lower figure gives the value of a third of the beat,

e.g. $\frac{6}{4}$ = 2 (6 ÷ 3) dotted minim beats in a bar.

9   *All* time signatures with 6, 9, 12, 15, or further multiples of three as the upper figure are *compound*.

10   $\frac{4}{4}$ time is often denoted by the symbol C:

This originated in medieval music where a circle ◯ was used to indicate triple (perfect) time, and an incomplete circle C duple time (imperfect). It is colloquially known as common time.

11 In similar fashion, $\frac{2}{2}$ time is often denoted by the symbol ¢:

He could well have written the same passage in notes half the length:

12 Music may be notated in different ways. If it contains a good deal of rapid divisions, these may be written as quavers rather than semiquavers in order to help the performer,
e.g. Haydn writes this in his Symphony No. 103 in E flat major:

He could well have written the same passage in notes half the length:

Both would sound the same, and composers are not consistent in their choice.

13 On the other hand, some composers preferred to write slow movements with a quaver beat, which often led to a dense proliferation of notes when subdivisions of the beat resulted in hemidemisemiquavers ( ) or even smaller note-values.

Beethoven: *Piano Concerto No. 3* (2nd movement)

The music is very slow and broad (*Largo*) and might equally well have been written like this with a crotchet beat:

H Mixed rhythms

1 In simple time, where a composer wishes to include a beat divided into three, he indicates the unusual division with a **triplet** sign. Now three quavers will be played in the time of two.

2 When in compound time a beat is divided equally into two instead of three, either a **duplet** sign is used:

or the two notes are dotted, thus:

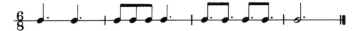

3   Any other unusual division is indicated in a similar way.

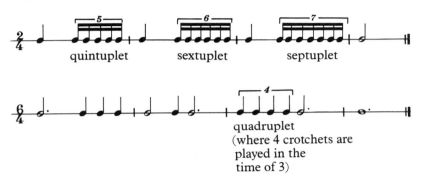

quintuplet   sextuplet   septuplet

quadruplet
(where 4 crotchets are
played in the
time of 3)

Annotated examples for I G and H

Bizet: *Carillon* from *L'Arlésienne*

1   Three crotchets in a bar = simple triple time.
2   Beat divided into three quavers in time of two = *triplet*.
3   Six quavers joined together. Common practice in $\frac{3}{4}$ time, but never in $\frac{6}{8}$.

Tchaikovsky: *Symphony No. 5* (2nd movement)

I H 1 to 3

1 Slow movement in $\frac{12}{8}$ time. Four dotted crotchets in a bar = compound quadruple time.
2 Tied notes equal to five quavers or 1⅔ beats.
3 Beat divided in two instead of three = *duplet*.
4 Normal 'compound' division of beat into three quavers.

Tchaikovsky: *Symphony No. 6* (2nd movement)

1 Quintuple time – five crotchet beats in a bar.
2 Triplet quavers.
3 First two bars repeated three notes higher in *sequence* (see II E17).
4 Tenor clef used to avoid leger lines.

Bartók: *Concerto for Orchestra*

(2nd movement)

(4th movement)

1 Unusual grouping of seven semiquavers: semiquaver rest completes two beats.
2 Triplet semiquavers equal one quaver.
3 Five semiquavers (quintuplet) in the time of four.
4 Alternating $\frac{2}{4}$ and $\frac{5}{8}$ time. $\frac{5}{8}$ groups into three and two quavers.
5 All quavers of equal length – not a triplet.

Brahms: *Symphony No. 3* (4th movement)

1 Key signature of four flats indicates A flat major or F minor (see I Q). Accidentals in this extract, in particular A and E naturals, change it to F major.
2 Tune on horns and cellos, mostly in triplet crotchets, sounding against two normal crotchets in bass – a favourite rhythmic device of Brahms.
3 Double basses and bassoons maintain steady four crotchets in a bar.
4 Triplet quavers on violins and violas.

J Anacrusis

1 Pieces of music tend to divide naturally into sections, similar to sentences or paragraphs in prose. These sections are called **phrases**.

2 Pieces or phrases do not necessarily start on the first beat of a bar.

Bach: *Suite for Orchestra No. 3* (5th movement)

The first note in the example above is called an upbeat, or **anacrusis**.

3 The same pattern of phrasing often continues throughout the piece; and the last bar, which is usually incomplete, complements the value of the opening upbeat (or beats) to make a complete bar.

Ibid.

[5 quavers only]

4 Certain old dance forms, such as the **gavotte**, start half-way through a $\frac{2}{2}$ or $\frac{4}{4}$ bar and the last bar is therefore also a half-bar.

Ibid. (3rd movement)

[2 crotchets]

(Ending)

[2 crotchets]

K Grouping of notes and rests

1 Notes should be grouped to show the natural divisions of the bar. In four-time, the middle of the bar should normally be apparent.

2 Notes of lesser value than a beat should be grouped together to make up one beat.

3 Quavers may be grouped in fours to form a half-bar, but generally not placed across the middle of the bar.

4 Six quavers may be grouped together in a whole $\frac{3}{4}$ bar, but not in a $\frac{6}{8}$ bar.

5 Similarly, in $\frac{3}{8}$ time, semiquavers may be grouped together.

Right   Wrong

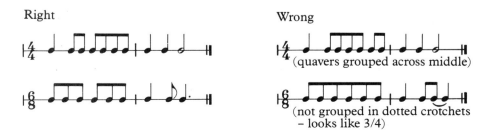

(quavers grouped across middle)

(not grouped in dotted crotchets – looks like 3/4)

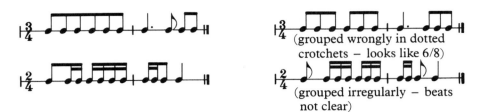

6 Occasionally irregular groupings may be encountered, especially in music from Eastern Europe (e.g. Bartók) and in music of Latin American origin. These types often contain a mixture of crotchet and dotted crotchet beats, grouped accordingly. Time signatures are usually expressed in *quavers* to accommodate both single and dotted beats.

Bartók: *String Quartet No. 5* (3rd movement)

7 Rests are grouped in a similar way. Single beats and half bars must be clear.

8 In quadruple time, a two-beat rest is used to complete either half of the bar. It may *never* be used on the second and third beats, across the middle of the bar.

9 A whole bar's rest is normally shown by a **semibreve rest**.
A rest of more than one bar is shown in one of the following ways:

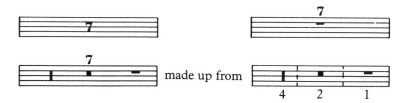

10 Completing the value of a beat in rests is not unlike the procedure used in giving change, where the sequence of 'rounding off' units starts with the smallest: e.g. when 36½p is spent from £1, ½p change makes it up to 37p, 1p makes 38p, 2p makes 40p, 10p added makes 50p and the outstanding half of the pound is completed with a 50p piece.

In simple time, imagine the beat divided into two, four, eight, or sixteen, then complete the smallest fraction with a rest to make it equivalent to the next largest and so on.

A demisemiquaver is ⅛ of a crotchet beat.

Add a demisemiquaver rest to make a quarter of a beat,

and the next largest rest to make up half the beat.

Now complete the beat by adding a quaver rest.

The remainder of the ⁴₄ bar is completed with a crotchet and a minim rest.

11 In compound time, imagine the beat divided into three, six, twelve or twenty-four and proceed as above, except that the value of the *note* must be completed before adding a rest for the *dot*.

crotchet | dot

Imagine beats subdivided
into six.

Add a semiquaver rest to
complete first quaver.

Add a quaver rest to
equal crotchet.

Add a further quaver
rest for the dot.

Add two dotted crotchet
rests to complete bar.
(*Not* a dotted minim rest
for the two beats combined.)

It is vital that the rest for the dot should always be shown.

this: not this:

and this: not this:

Some composers and publishers prefer to replace the dot in a one-beat rest with
an additional rest.

12 When a fraction of a beat is preceded by a rest, reverse the procedure used in
10 and 11 to complete a beat.

Note that for the first and second subdivisions of the beat, a crotchet rest is correct, *not* two quavers.

13 In section B it was seen that the first beat of a bar, and to a lesser degree the third beat of a quadruple bar, is stressed or **accented**. Sometimes, however, a beat or part of a beat other than the first is also accented, giving a **syncopated** effect. Such exceptional accents are notated as follows:

14 **Syncopation** occurs in three contexts:

a Where a weak beat is accented:

(Haydn)

b Where an accented beat is silent, thereby throwing the stress onto a subsequent beat:

(Chopin)

c Where a long note starts on a weak beat or part of a beat and extends into the next beat.
When this happens in quadruple time, the principle that the middle of the bar should be clearly shown is sometimes abandoned in favour of a simpler representation with fewer notes, e.g. ♩ ♩ ♩ rather than ♩ ♩ ♩ ♩

(Bach)

15 As an exercise, you are sometimes asked to add bar-lines and a time signature to an unbarred passage. When working such an exercise look out for:

a the total number of beats, which might exclude the possibility of certain times

b any regular rhythmic patterns which might form bars

c any long notes which must fit within a single bar or form a final bar

d any tied notes which might occur across a bar line (*or* which might come in the middle of a four- or six-time bar; *or* which, if at the end, might indicate an incomplete bar requiring a complementary anacrusis)

e signs of simple time such as groups of twos or fours and any dotted notes followed by single quavers or other groups equal to the value of the dot

f signs of compound time such as groups of threes, dotted notes and units made of unequal values, especially crotchets followed by single quavers.

Here are two examples:

1

a a count of crotchet beats gives 16, which excludes triple time

b there are no groups of threes, so compound time is unlikely

c the one dotted note is followed by a note of the value of the dot, i.e. a quaver

d the quavers form a group of four, not of three

e it looks like simple time – two or four crotchets in a bar

f the two-beat note at the end might be a complete bar, but a count-back in bars of two crotchets results in the second note of the passage being cut in two by a bar-line

g an anacrusis might be considered, but then the quaver group would occur across the middle of a bar

h therefore, barring in four crotchets must be correct, with an example of syncopation in the first bar.

(There is no certain way of distinguishing between $\frac{4}{4}$ and $\frac{2}{2}$ as this would depend on tempo markings and in some cases on implied harmony.)

a there are the equivalents of 12 crotchets, making two-, three-, or four-time possible

b ♩. ♫ looks like ⁶⁄₈ time but is sometimes incorrectly or confusingly used in ³⁄₄ instead of ♩. ♪♫

c ♪♩ ♩ ♪ is a syncopation which could come in ⁶⁄₈ or ³⁄₄

d ♩. ♫ ♫ the dotted note is followed by a pattern equal to the dot and then by a pair of quavers – a strong indication of simple time: this rhythm in ⁶⁄₈ would be grouped ♩. ♫♫

e ♩ ♪ at the end looks like an incomplete bar – added to the odd quaver at the beginning, it equals three beats; a five-quaver sound in ⁶⁄₈ would have been written as ♩ ♩

f so the first quaver is an anacrusis

g an attempt to bar in two- or four-time leads to a split note or group within a few beats

h therefore the piece must be in ³⁄₄.

Annotated examples for I K

Vaughan Williams: *Symphony No. 6* (3rd movement)

1 Change of time.
2 *Tenuto* or *marcato* marks for emphasis.
3 Four quavers joined in straightforward bar.

4 Tie across bar.
5 Each beat clearly defined.

Elgar: *Enigma Variations* (No. 5, 'R.P.A.')

Ibid. (No. 10, 'Dorabella')

1 Four dotted crotchet beats clearly displayed.
2 Acciaccatura or 'crushed' note.
3 First phrase repeated five notes higher in sequential manner (see II E17).
4 Further sequential treatment, characteristic of Elgar.
5 Half bar rest in compound quadruple time.
6 Third beat of bar shown with quaver rest for value of dot.
7 Rhythmic details clarified by divisions of quavers, starting with quaver rest.
8 Quaver rest completes second beat.
9 Pizzicato – plucked not bowed.
10 With mutes (see V F11).
11 Three demisemiquavers followed by demisemiquaver rest – complete half-beat before addition of quaver rest.
12 Second beat crotchet rest, clearly separated from first beat.

L Intervals

1   It is necessary to have a system for identifying the distance, or **interval**, between any two notes.

2   Intervals are always calculated inclusively to include both the lower and upper notes.

3   They are named according to the number of letter names in their formation.

Key C

2nd	3rd	4th	5th	6th	7th	8ve (octave)
						C
					B	B
				A	A	A
			G	G	G	G
		F	F	F	F	F
	E	E	E	E	E	E
D	D	D	D	D	D	D
C	C	C	C	C	C	C

4   In addition, they are given a qualifying name according to their precise size. In the major scale, the intervals made by each note with the tonic are as follows:

major 2nd   major 3rd   perfect 4th   perfect 5th   major 6th   major 7th

Notice here that most of the intervals are *major*, although the term *major* in this context is best thought of as an indication of size. The two perfect intervals are so-called because the simple ratio between the vibrating frequencies of the two notes results in a pure, open sound (see the comments on the **harmonic series** in Chapter II). For this reason, the *unison*, when two voices or parts sing the same note, and the *octave* are both perfect intervals, but the term 'perfect' is not necessarily added when describing them.

5   The form of an interval is changed when one or both of its sounds is raised (*sharpened*) or lowered (*flattened*) by one or two semitones, *without* changing their letter names.

6 Major intervals become *minor* (i.e. smaller) when reduced by a semitone.

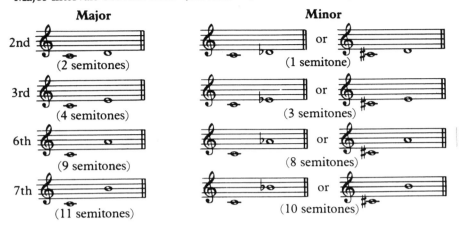

7 Perfect intervals become **diminished** (i.e. smaller) when reduced by a semitone,

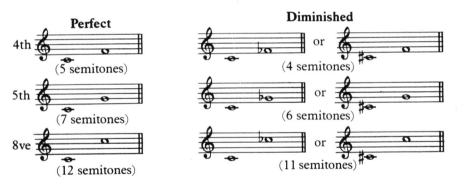

and **augmented** (i.e. bigger) when extended by a semitone.

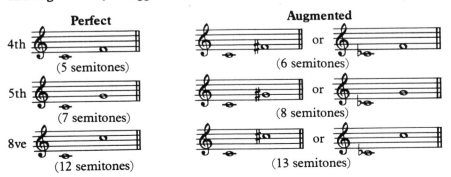

8 Major 2nds and 6ths become *augmented* when extended by a semitone, without changing the letter names.

NB Augmented 3rds and 7ths are not found in common musical usage.

9 Minor 3rds and 7ths become *diminished* when reduced by a further semitone, while retaining their original letter names.

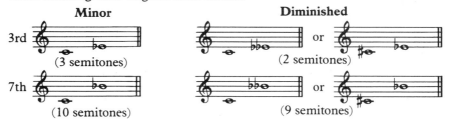

NB Diminished 2nds and 6ths are not found in common musical usage.

10 The table below summarizes the forms in which intervals may occur.

Interval		Forms (in ascending order of size)		
2nd	(diminished)	minor	major	augmented
3rd	diminished	minor	major	(augmented)
4th	diminished		perfect	augmented
5th	diminished		perfect	augmented
6th	(diminished)	minor	major	augmented
7th	diminished	minor	major	(augmented)
8th	diminished		perfect	augmented

Notice that many interval sizes can be described in more than one way, e.g. a major 2nd is the same size (two semitones) as a diminished 3rd. The correct description depends on the notation used (C – D is a major 2nd, C – E double flat a diminished 3rd), and this in turn depends on the key of the music. This dual description affects particularly the augmented 4th/diminished 5th (C – F sharp/G flat), the only interval size which can't be described in any way as minor, major or perfect.

11 When an interval has a compass greater than an octave, it is called a **compound interval**. This indicates that it is made up of two smaller intervals, the lower of which is always an octave.

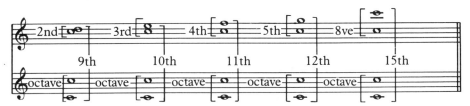

Because the two intervals making up a compound interval overlap, the numerical size of the resultant interval is one degree less than the sum of the two together, e.g. a 10th is made up of an octave and a 3rd ($10 = 8 + 3 - 1$).

Compound intervals can also be major, minor, perfect, diminished or augmented: this depends on their upper constituent intervals.

12 To name an interval, first count the number of letter names from the lower to the upper note inclusively. Then, whenever possible, take the lower note as the tonic of a major scale (irrespective of the key of the passage in which the interval occurs).

This interval is some form of 6th. Taking the bottom note (G) as the tonic, then the major 6th above G is E natural. But the given interval to be named is G – E flat and is therefore one semitone less, i.e. a minor 6th.

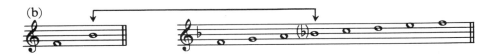

Count the letter names – this interval is some form of 4th. Taking the bottom note (F) as the tonic, then the perfect 4th above F is B flat. But the given interval is F – B natural, and is therefore one semitone larger, i.e. an augmented 4th.

(c)

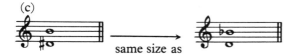

same size as

Count the letter names – this interval is some form of 6th. In this case, the lower note (D sharp) is not the tonic of a standard major scale (do not think of it as E flat). The easiest way to deal with this is to lower *both* notes by a semitone, while maintaining both letter names. A major 6th up from D is B natural, but the top note of our adjusted interval is B flat, so the interval is a minor 6th.

13 Any interval can be turned upside down, or **inverted**, by transposing the lower note one or more octaves upwards, so that the original note becomes the bass, or by transposing the upper note *down* in a similar way.

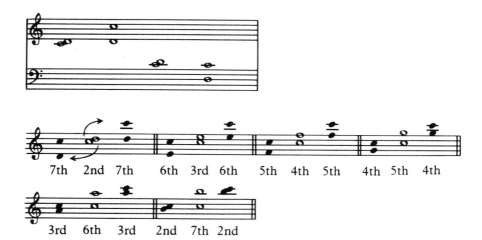

In each case the original interval added to the inverted interval has a numerical value of nine (not eight as might be expected with an octave transposition) because both intervals are counted inclusively, which means that the stationary note is counted twice.

Furthermore, with the exception of perfect intervals which remain perfect, inverted intervals change their form.

A perfect 4th becomes a perfect 5th and a perfect 5th becomes a perfect 4th,

but major intervals become minor,

Major 3rd Minor 6th Major 2nd Minor 7th

and minor intervals become major,

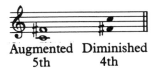

Minor 3rd Major 6th Minor 2nd Major 7th

augmented intervals become diminished,

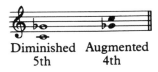

Augmented   Diminished
    5th   4th

and diminished intervals become augmented.

Diminished Augmented
    5th   4th

This provides us with an alternative method of describing intervals with awkward lower notes, such as we saw in example 12 (c) above. If we invert the interval,

the result is a major third, and from the above examples we know that the inversion of a major 3rd is a minor 6th (3 + 6 = 9, major becomes minor).

14 The fashion for what is accepted as pleasing to the ear changes continually. However, major and minor 3rds and 6ths, and perfect 5ths and octaves, have always been considered stable and consonant, while perfect 4ths, as well as major and minor 2nds and 7ths, are considered unstable, or dissonant.

15 *Augmented 4ths* or *diminished 5ths* are sometimes referred to as *tritones* because they span three whole tones. The tritone is characterized by its highly unstable quality, and has proved a source of attraction for some composers during the last hundred years. It is also a principal component of the important **dominant 7th** chord, around which the harmonic system used from c.1600 to c.1900 was built (see II C).

Annotated examples for I L

Britten: *Serenade for tenor, horn and strings* (Prologue)

* The Prologue to be played on natural harmonics.

1 Horn in F. Sounds a fifth lower than written.
Solo instrument – all intervals are melodic.
2 No time signature, since number of crotchets in bar varies.

3   Perfect 5th.
4   Comma indicates break in pulse.
5   Tone or major 2nd.
6   Major 3rd.
7   Perfect 4th.
8   Minor 3rd.
9   Minor 7th.
10   Major 6th.
11   Major 10th or compound major 3rd.

Ibid. (Elegy)

12   Horn in F. Sounds a fifth lower than written.
13   Key signature for B minor. Horns usually written without key signature.
14   Chromatic semitone.
15   Octave.
16   Diatonic semitone.
17   Confirmatory accidental. Bass has conflicting note.

Grieg: *Waltz, Op. 12 No. 2* (from bar 11)

1 Major 6th.
2 Minor 6th.
3 Perfect 4th.
4 Augmented 4th.
5 Sequence – bars 1 and 2 repeated a 3rd lower.
6 Perfect 5th followed by a diminished 5th.
7 Chord spanning an octave made up from a perfect 5th and a perfect 4th.

Schoenberg: *6 kleine Klavierstücke* (No. 3)

1 Atonal music (i.e. without key or tonal centre), so many cautionary accidentals.
2 Minor 7th.
3 Right hand chord spanning a major 7th, made up from a perfect 4th and an augmented 4th.
4 Minor 6th.
5 Diminished 5th.
6 Major 7ths – melodic in right hand, harmonic in left hand.
7 Three quavers – not a triplet.
8 D sharp and E flat – same note written in two ways – **enharmonic** notation.
9 Augmented 6th.
10 Single G continues after two staccato chords.

M Minor scales

1 Apart from the major scale, the other scale in common use is called the **minor scale**. The minor scale is less bright than the major and is therefore often used for music of a serious or melancholy nature.

2 The simplest minor scale is that starting on A. It corresponds to the major scale of C in having no flats or sharps in its key signature.

3 However, the minor scale is never used in this basic form – the seventh note is usually raised by a semitone so that it leads to the tonic. In this form it is called the **harmonic minor scale**.

Note that the G sharp is an *accidental*, and not part of the key signature.

4 Comparing the A harmonic minor scale with the A major scale, only two notes are different – instead of a major 3rd (A – C sharp), there is a minor 3rd (A – C natural), and instead of a major 6th (A – F sharp), there is a minor 6th (A – F natural). So whether a piece is major or minor depends on the 3rd and the 6th.

5 The harmonic minor scale has a characteristic interval between the sixth and the seventh degrees of an *augmented 2nd*. This sounds awkward, especially when sung, and to avoid this the sixth note of the scale is sometimes raised together with the seventh. This form is known as the **melodic minor scale**.

When there is no need for a raised seventh, e.g. when singing down the scale, the accidentals in the melodic minor scale are omitted and the scale reverts to its basic minor form.

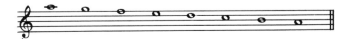

6 Each major scale has a corresponding minor scale known as its **relative minor** with the same number of sharps or flats in the key signature. As with A minor to C major, the tonic of the relative minor scale is a minor 3rd below the tonic of the major.

7 So there are 12 distinct minor scales. Notice that the scales of D sharp minor and E flat minor (which are very rarely encountered) sound the same, like their relative majors F sharp/G flat.

The *harmonic minor* forms are shown below.

8 The *relative minor* tonic is the submediant note or sixth degree of the major scale.

Conversely, the *relative major* tonic is the mediant or third degree of the minor scale.

9 Notice also that when an already flat seventh is raised (as in F minor), a natural is used. When raising a seventh which is already sharp (as in G sharp minor), a double sharp is used.

10 Although not related by key signature, major and minor scales on the *same* tonic are frequently associated. Composers such as Haydn delighted in composing sets of variations which alternated between the major and tonic minor keys.

11 To change any major scale into its tonic harmonic minor, lower by a semitone the third and sixth notes. Leave the seventh note (which is already a leading note) unchanged.

a G major

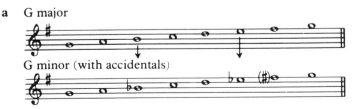

Then move the accidentals to a key signature and sharpen the seventh note.

G minor (with a key signature)

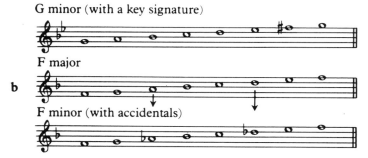

F major

F minor (with accidentals)

b

Construct a key signature by adding the missing ringed flat and then cancelling with a natural.

F minor (with key signature)

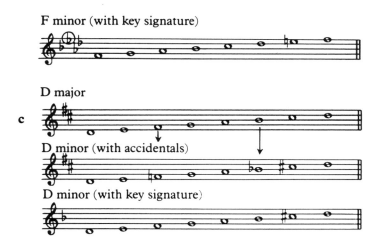

D major

D minor (with accidentals)

D minor (with key signature)

c

12 When a major scale is changed to an ascending melodic minor, only the third degree is lowered as the upper tetrachord remains exactly the same. In the descending form the complete minor key signature is restored.

B flat major

B flat melodic minor (with accidental)

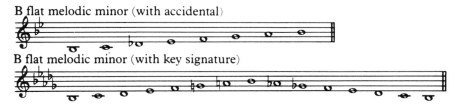

B flat melodic minor (with key signature)

N Modes

1. Our system of major and minor scales evolved from a series of scales called **modes**.

2. Modes were in general use in Western European music until about 1600 and still survive in plainsong and folk music. There were altogether seven so-called **authentic** modes, each beginning with a different note within the compass corresponding to the white notes on a piano from C to C. The lowest note of each authentic mode was known as the **final**.

   Each mode derives its character from the position of the semitone steps (bracketed in the examples below) in its formation and from the interval content in relation to its final.

Ionian mode

Our major scale in the key of C.

Dorian mode

Common in our folk heritage, characteristic intervals from final, minor 3rd and major 6th.

Phrygian mode

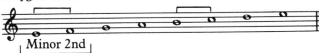

Rare in Western music, characteristic interval a semitone or minor 2nd between final and 2nd degrees.

Lydian mode

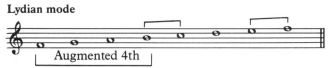

Augmented 4th

Prominent in Polish folk music, characteristic interval an augmented 4th above final.

Mixolydian mode

whole tone

Important in jazz, like a major scale without a leading note semitone.

Aeolian mode

Minor 3rd Minor 6th

The direct ancestor of our minor scale, characteristic intervals minor 3rd and minor 6th from final.

Locrian

Diminished 5th

Only mode with a diminished 5th between its final and 5th degrees. Until the 20th century, when its unstable quality attracted some composers, it remained a largely theoretical mode.

3   Except for the Ionian (major scale) and the Lydian (with its characteristic augmented 4th), no mode has a leading note effect between the seventh and eighth notes.

Dorian, Phrygian, Mixolydian and Aeolian modes all have whole tones between their seventh and eighth notes. As certain harmonic progressions became more common, the need to raise the seventh note in every mode led to their eclipse by the beginning of the 17th century.

4   Dorian, Phrygian and Aeolian modes all have a minor 3rd between their first and third notes, giving them a minor quality. Ionian, Lydian and Mixolydian have a major third between these degrees.

O Chromatic and other scales

1　In the European musical tradition, three other scales are occasionally used besides those already studied.

2　Of these, the most common is the **chromatic scale** which consists of 12 semi-tone steps from a note to its octave.

3　In its academic form it is written by combining the notes of the major and minor scales:

and then adding a sharpened subdominant and a flattened supertonic.

This is called a **harmonic chromatic scale** and has 12 different notes. Notice that all the letter-names appear *twice* apart from the tonic and dominant.

4　However, in practice, composers generally write the scale in the most convenient and easily-read form, sharpening notes on the way up and flattening them when descending.

The underlying harmonic structure (see Chapter II) may also influence notation.

5　The **pentatonic scale**, as its name implies, is a scale with five different notes. It is often found in folk-music and, in its most usual form, can be regarded as a gapped major scale, with the interval of a minor 3rd occurring between the third and fifth, and sixth and eighth degrees.

The scale is that one produced on the piano by playing the black notes only. The lack of semitones and the preponderance of tones and minor 3rds give it its characteristic quality.

6 The **whole-tone scale** consists entirely of major 2nd steps and occurs in only two forms, one beginning on C and the other on D flat (or C sharp). It has some affinity with scales used in the Far East and its use by some 20th-century composers, notably Debussy, is often evocative. It is tonally ambiguous, being composed entirely of equal intervals with no semitones.

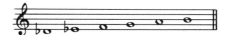

Annotated examples for I M, N and O

English Folk Song: *The Bonny Labouring Boy*

1 Open key signature – C major, A minor or mode?
2 First bar establishes dominant-tonic outline with D as keynote.
3 Minor 3rd above D points to minor scale or mode.
4 Flat 7th or whole tone below D indicates mode.
5 Major 6th above D confirms Dorian mode.

English Carol: *God Rest You Merry, Gentlemen*

1   First bar outlines tonic-dominant with E as keynote.
2   Minor 3rd above E points to minor scale or mode.
3   Flat 7th indicates mode.
4   C natural, minor 6th above E confirms Aeolian mode.

   Note that in both examples the sixth above the tonic does not occur until after
the first phrase, delaying the confirmation of Dorian (major 6th) or Aeolian
(minor 6th). Many songs with otherwise minor modal characteristics do not
contain a sixth degree, making the actual mode equivocal. Some tunes, like
Greensleeves, include both a minor 6th (in the first half) and a major 6th (in the
second half).

Chopin: *Mazurka Op. 68 No. 3*

1   Tonic-dominant drone continues throughout in left hand.
2   E naturals throughout cancel key signature and produce an augmented 4th
    above B flat.
3   Recurring augmented 4th indicates influence of Lydian mode.

Bach: *Harpsichord Concerto in D minor* (BWV 1052) (1st movement)

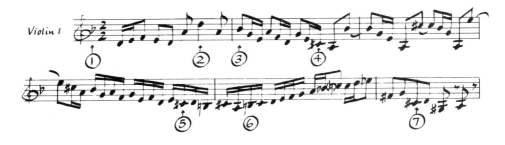

Ibid. (2nd movement)

Violin I

1   Key signature of one flat – either F major or D minor.
2   D and A prominent in first bar, i.e. tonic and dominant in D minor, pointing
     to D minor.
3   Melodic line derived from broken chords (see Chapter II).
4   First of a number of C sharps in extract, confirming D minor not F major.
5   C sharp and associated B natural – melodic minor element.
6   D minor melodic scale.
7   Accidentals F sharp, C sharp and G sharp emphasize their succeeding notes a
     semitone higher.
8   Key signature of two flats, either B flat major or G minor, but opening
     proclaims G minor.
9   Two notes taken in one bow stroke, not a tie.
10   Melodic line derived from a chordal pattern.
11   F sharp leading note in G minor.
12   Rising neighbouring-note figure at beginning of this and next two bars.

Negro Spiritual: *Deep River*

1   E flat major key signature.
2   Preponderance of minor 3rds and major 2nds points to pentatonic idiom.
3   No semitonic movement arising from leading note, since this seventh degree, together with the fourth degree, is absent from the pentatonic.

Dvořák: *Symphony No. 9 in E minor* (New World) (2nd movement)

1   Key of D flat major, but melody basically pentatonic.
2   Characteristic pentatonic intervals, minor 3rds and major 2nds.
3   Middle four bars include C, the leading note in the key of D flat, but it avoids any semitone leading movement direct to the tonic.
4   Remaining four bars use only the notes of the pentatonic scale.

Debussy: *Voiles* (Préludes, Book 1)

1 Melody moves by whole-tone steps.
2 Major 3rds characteristic of whole tone scale.
3 Only the notes C, D, E, F sharp, A flat and B flat used, confirming the whole tone scale. With the exception of the middle section (which is pentatonic) and one small digression, the entire piece is based on these six notes – rare even in Debussy.
4 B flat continues in low part throughout the piece. Technically known as a **pedal point** (see V C9).

P Placing intervals

1 You sometimes need to know in which keys a given interval may occur.

2 Any major, minor or perfect interval will occur in a number of keys, but diminished and augmented intervals are much more restricted in context.

3 The examples below show how this exercise may be approached.

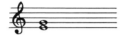 In how many major and harmonic minor keys does this interval occur?

This interval is a minor 3rd.
  Investigate the major scales first. For simplicity, take C major as a starting point and look at all the thirds occurring in that scale:

major   minor   minor   major   major   minor   minor

There are four minor 3rds, the lower notes being, respectively, the second, third, sixth, and seventh degrees of the scale. So, returning to our original interval (E – G), this will occur in the major scales for which E (the bottom note) is the second, the third, the sixth, and the seventh – so the tonics will be found a major 2nd, a major 3rd, a major 6th, and a major 7th below E – in other words D major, C major, G major, and F major.
  Now investigate the harmonic minor scales. Again, take A minor as a starting point and look at all the thirds occurring in that scale:

minor   minor   major   minor   major   major   minor

Here again there are four minor thirds, the lower notes being respectively the tonic, the second, the fourth and the seventh degrees of the scale. So our original interval will occur in the minor scales for which E is the tonic, the second, the fourth and the seventh – so the tonics will be found on E and then a major 2nd, perfect 4th and major 7th below E, in other words E minor, D minor, B minor, and F minor.

So E – G occurs in eight scales: D major, C major, G major, F major, D minor, B minor, E minor, and F minor.

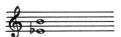

This is an augmented 5th.

Again, look first at the major scale. Take C major as the basis and look at all the fifths occurring in that scale.

perfect   perfect   perfect   perfect   perfect   perfect diminished

So the augmented 5th does not occur in any major scale. Now look at the minor scales. The fifths occurring in A minor are shown below:

perfect diminished augmented perfect   perfect   perfect diminished

There is *one* augmented 5th only, its lower note being the third degree of the scale. Returning to the original interval (E flat – B), we can say it occurs in just one minor scale, for which E flat is the mediant, i.e. C minor (harmonic).

Q Finding the key of a passage

1   The following section gives some guidelines for the identification of the key of a passage or a piece of music. The method depends on whether the passage has a key signature.

2   If it *has* a key signature:
    a Count the number of sharps or flats and check against the **Key Signature Table** on page 19. This will give two possibilities: a major key or its relative minor.

b Check the passage for the presence of accidentals or chromatic alterations. If the seventh degree of what would be the relative minor scale is consistently raised, this indicates the minor key.

c As a further check, look for emphasis on tonic and dominant notes.

(i)   Mozart: *Concerto for two pianos K365* (1st movement)

a Key signature of three flats, implies E flat major or C minor.

b If C minor, B flats would have to be raised to B naturals, but this is not the case.

c Check. Note the predominance of the tonic (E flat) and the dominant (B flat), confirming key of E flat major.

(ii)   Bach: *Mass in B minor* (No. 10, Qui sedes)

a Key signature of two sharps, implies D major or B minor.

b If B minor, A's would have to be raised to A sharps, which is indeed the case.

c Check. Note the stress on the tonic (B) and the dominant (F sharp), confirming the key of B minor.

NB The A natural in the last complete bar occurs as a result of the descending melodic form of the minor scale.

3 If the passage has *no* key signature work out which notes carry accidentals and compare them with the standard sequence of sharps and flats.
The examples below illustrate this procedure:

(i)   Schubert: *Piano Sonata in A minor* (1st movement)

a Two notes are flattened – E flat and A flat.
b The order in which flats arise is B flat – E flat – A flat – D flat.
c So this passage has the second and third flats, but not the first. The presence of the second and third, but no subsequent flats in the sequence suggests the scale with three flats – E flat major or C minor.
d But there is an apparent problem – namely the lack of B flats.
e But in C minor the seventh degree is raised (B flat to B), so the passage is clearly in C minor.
f Notice that, while this passage is in C minor, the work itself is in A minor. Large-scale works usually contain passages not in the tonic key (this movement from one key to another within a piece is called **modulation**, see Chapter II). Do not be misled by any key mentioned in the title, as the passage may be taken from a section which has *modulated*.

(ii)   Mozart: *String Quartet in C, K465* (3rd movement)

a In the *first* phrase, two notes are sharpened – D sharp and G sharp.
b The order in which sharps arise is F sharp, C sharp, G sharp, D sharp and A sharp.
c The presence of D sharp but also A natural in the example suggests the key of E major, confirmed by the importance of the dominant (B) and tonic (E).
d But, in the second phrase, G sharp reverts to G natural, suggesting the key of E *minor*.
  Again, this is a passage from a longer work, which is actually in the key of C major. The short phrases above are in E major and then E minor, but this may not be important in the context of the piece as a whole – they can be thought of as passing modulations.

4   When a passage includes chromatic notes, look out for their possible relation-ship to degrees of the scale as **decorative notes**. These decorative chromatic notes will usually be a semitone away from their associated diatonic notes and, most commonly, a semitone *below* as in the following passage, which is not in D major (two sharps), but in C major. Harmonic knowledge will clarify these more complex passages.

Haydn: *String Quartet Op. 54 No. 2*

R Signs and abbreviations

1 A **double bar** indicates the end of a movement or section and in classical or post-classical music it is used when a change of time-signature occurs.

2 A double bar preceded by two or four dots signifies that the music is to be repeated: repetition takes place from a previous double bar with dots to the right or from the beginning of the movement.

3 Variation of the termination of a passage on repetition is shown thus:

On repetition, the second-time bar is to be played instead of the preceding one.

4 The letters D.C. (Da Capo) and D.$. (Dal Segno) are also used to indicate a *repeat*.

D.C. means repeat from the beginning and continue to the word *Fine* (or to a 'hold' ⌢ , which is sometimes substituted for *Fine*).

D.$. means repeat from the point marked with the sign 𝄋 and continue to the word *Fine*.

5   A *pause*, ∩ , written over or under a note or rest means that the note or rest is
    to be prolonged at the discretion of the performer. If a considerable pause is
    intended, the words *Lunga Pausa* are used.

    The letters G.P. are used in orchestral music to signify silence for the whole
    orchestra.

6   *8va*, with or without a dotted line, means that a passage is to be played an
    octave higher than written. Resumption of ordinary pitch is indicated by the
    cessation of the dotted line or by the word *loco*.

Chopin: *Ballade in G minor*

    8va bassa, or *8va sotto*, written under the notes of the bass stave, signifies that
    they are to be played an octave lower.

    8ves (*Con 8*, or *8*) means that a passage is to be played in octaves.

7   A *slur*, ⌒ or ⌣ , written above or below two or more consecutive notes indi-
    cates that they are to be played in a smooth, connected manner, with an almost
    imperceptible shortening of the last note. It is also used:

    a To mark the phrasing.

Beethoven: *Piano Sonata in F minor Op. 2 No. 1*

    b To indicate notes sung to a single syllable in vocal music.

Bach: *Mass in B minor*

Glo - - ri - a in - ex - cel(-sis)

c (i) To indicate the bowing of a string passage. Notes written with a slur are to be played with one bow, i.e. one *stroke* of a bow.

Handel: *Violin Sonata in A*

(ii) To indicate the tonguing of a wind passage. Only the first note written within a slur is 'attacked', and the others are played without a further tongue movement.

Wagner: *Flying Dutchman*

Oboe

(iii) To show (for a keyboard or wind instrument) that the notes are to be played without a perceptible break between them.

Ibid.

Bassoon

8 Notes played in a short detached manner produce the effect of *staccato*. The three grades of staccato are:
a *Staccato*

Schumann: *Fughetta*

b *Staccatissimo*

Brahms: *Piano Sonata, Op. 2*

As short and as detached as possible.

c *Mezzo staccato*

Brahms: *String Sextet*

Half staccato, with slight stress
on the marked notes (see below).

9 The *marcato* or *tenuto* sign (–) under or over a note indicates slightly more than
the normal stress.

Mahler: *Symphony No. 4 in G*

Or as a cautionary reminder that that note is not staccato.

10 Sforzando (*sf* or *fz*)

Emphasis upon a particular note is shown by means of a sign > or ∧ written
above it. A short, forceful accent on a given note is called *sforzando* and is
indicated by the letters *sf* or *fz* above it.

11 Repeated notes

(i) A note written with one or more strokes above it or through its stem is to be
repeated instead of being held. The *number* of strokes signifies the frequency
of reiteration – one stroke representing quavers, two strokes semiquavers,
etc.; the *value* of the written note represents the duration of reiteration.

Written   Played

(ii) Rapid alternation of *two* notes is expressed thus:

Written   Played

a

Written   Played

b

The *duration* of the alternation is expressed by the written note, the *speed* by the number of strokes. Note that the total value of the semiquavers in each example equals *one* only of the written notes.

12 Tremolando

Notes to be alternated or reiterated as quickly as possible are written thus:

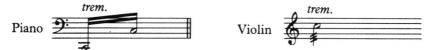

13 Signs for repeated groups of notes

One stroke signifies repetition of the preceding group of quavers, *two* strokes represent a group of semiquavers.

The repetition of a group of notes in free time (often required in contemporary music exploring the possibilities of chance combination of sounds) is shown like this:

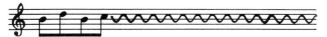

(The pattern is continued in relation to other instruments in the score, until the end of the wavy line.)

Repetition of the previous bar, or part of a bar, is indicated thus:

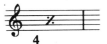   or

Further repetition of the same bar is indicated by adding a figure for the number of times it is to be played:

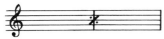

Or alternatively the repeat sign is spread over two bars:

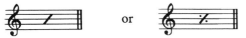

14 Arpeggio

In an arpeggio the notes of a chord are played in rapid succession upwards or downwards, each note, when sounded, being held for the remaining duration of the written note. The sign is a vertical undulating line (⁝) placed before the written notes of the chord.

There are three forms of arpeggio in common use:

15 Glissando

An indication to play, as rapidly as possible, all the notes which lie between those shown. In practice, some notes may be left out.

Usually the effect obtained is an approximation, e.g. keyboard players play only on white notes (or, rarely, black notes), not chromatically, while string players do not necessarily play across the complete compass marked, if it involves shifting across several strings. Trombones and pedal timpani are able to perform perfect glissandos, and, like harps, are especially associated with this technique.

S Ornaments

1 Introduction

In the Baroque and early Classical periods, i.e. from the early 17th century to the late 18th, it was the practice to grace or embellish a melody with appropriate ornaments even when no written indication was given by the composer. This taste for decoration paralleled the love of elaborate embellishment of architectural features in the Baroque era and reflected some of the grace and elegance in dress and manners of the Classical period.

During these periods, many attempts were made to rationalize the practice, which varied considerably from time to time and from one country to another.

The realizations listed here give only a general indication in line with the most common practice. In the Baroque era especially, emphasis was placed on rhythmic freedom, with an expressive 'leaning' on the first note (which invariably occurred *on* the beat rather than before it).

2 Appoggiatura

3 Acciaccatura

or  if in
quick tempo

4 Mordents

or ... when fast

or rarely in the 17th
and 18th centuries,
though common in
the 19th (e.g. in Chopin)

5 Trills or shakes
Until the 19th century it was customary to begin the trill on the upper
(auxiliary) note. After a number of alternations with the auxiliary note, the principal note might be dwelt upon.

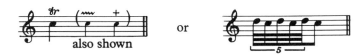

also shown   or

or 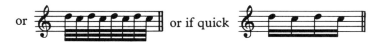 or if quick

By about the middle of the 18th century, whether indicated or not, an 'after-turn' or *Nachschlag* (German) might be used to complete the trill.

 or

Sometimes a trill might begin with a prefix from above or below.

When an ornamented note was approached from its upper neighbour, a break in legato could be avoided by means of a **tie**.

François Couperin and several other composers specifically indicated this practice by a slur.

6   Turns

When the prefix to a trill is isolated, it is known as a **turn**.

Turn

or in quick
tempo

Inverted turn

or in quick
tempo

Turn after a note

or in quick
tempo

Turn after a dotted note

or in quick
tempo

or in compound time

19th-century turn starting on the principal note

The same turn in earlier notation would be indicated like this:

T Terms used in music

Most terms used in music of all nationalities are written in *Italian*.

1 Tempo indications

Adagio Leisurely but not so slow as *Largo*
Allegro Quick, lively
Allegretto Less quickly than *Allegro*
Andante Going easily at a moderate pace
Andantino Strictly a somewhat *slower* rate than *Andante* but used
   generally to signify a pace somewhat faster than *Andante*
Grave Very slow, solemn
Largamente In a broad style; similar in meaning to *Largo*
Largo Broad, stately, and very slow
Larghetto Slow, but not so slow as *Largo*
Lento Slower than *Andante*, but not so slow as *Largo*
Moderato At a moderate pace
Presto Quicker than *Allegro*
Prestissimo Very quickly
Tempo comodo At an easy, conveneint pace
Tempo ordinario At a moderate pace
Vivo, Vivace Lively, briskly
Met. An indication of speed as shown by the **metronome**.
   Met. 60, or MM = 60, represents sixty pulses (beats) a minute.
   MM = *Maelzel's Metronome*

2 Tempo changes

Accelerando (*accel.*) Getting gradually quicker
Ad libitum, A piacere The manner of performance (pace, etc.) being
   left to the discretion of the performer
Allargando Decreasing in speed, broadening
A tempo, Tempo Returning to normal time
Calando Gradually decreasing in pace and tone

Doppio movimento Double the speed

L'istesso tempo Used sometimes with a change of time-signature, e.g. $\frac{2}{2} - \frac{2}{4}$, to indicate that the value of each *beat* remains the same in the new time as in the old

Meno allegro Less quickly

Meno mosso With less movement; slackening in pace

Morendo Dying away

Perdendosi Dying away (literally 'losing itself')

Più mosso With more movement; quickening

Ritardando (*ritard.*) Holding back, i.e. slow down gently

Rallentando (*rall.*) Getting gradually slower

Ritenuto (*rit.*) Hold back immediately

Smorzando See *Calando*

Stretto }
Stringendo } Increasing the pace

Tempo primo Returning to the original pace

Tempo giusto In exact time

Tempo rubato Allowing the performer freedom to lengthen and shorten notes (more or less imperceptibly) with a view to securing elasticity of line or of phrase, literally 'robbed time'

3   Performance practice

A In, according to

A cappella Unaccompanied (in reference to voices)

Affettuoso Tenderly, with feeling

Agitato Agitated, restless

Amabile Tenderly, gently

Amoroso In a gentle style (literally 'lovingly')

Animato With spirit, or with animation

Appassionato, -a; *Con passione* Impassioned, with deep feeling

Assai Very

Attacca Proceed immediately

Ben Well

Ben marcato Well marked

Brillante Brilliantly

Cantabile, Cantando In a singing style

Col or *Colla* With the . . .

Colla voce Following the solo part closely

Con With

Con brio With vigour

Con forza With force
Con fuoco With fire
Con grazia Gracefully, elegantly
Con moto With movement
Da capo al fine (Repeat) from the beginning, and end at the word 'Fine'
Dal segno (D.$.) Return to the sign
Dolce Sweetly
Dolente, Doloroso Sadly, plaintively
E or *Ed* And
Espressivo With expression
Fuoco Fire
Furioso Impetuously, wildly
Giocoso, Giocosamente Playfully, jocosely
Grazioso Gracefully
Legato Smoothly
Leggiero, Leggieramente Lightly
Lusingando Soothingly
Ma But
Maestoso With dignity, majestically
Meno Less
Mesto Sadly
Mezzo Half, e.g. *Mezzo forte* Moderately loud
Molto Very; *Di molto* Extremely
Mosso Moved cf. *Meno* and *Più*
Movimento Speed; *Doppio movimento* Twice as fast
Non Not
Non Tanto Not so much
Non troppo Not too much
Pesante Heavily
Piacevole Pleasantly, smoothly
Piangevole Sadly, plaintively
Più More
Poco Little, slightly
Poco a poco Little by little
Poi Then
Poi la coda Then to the Coda
Pomposo Pompously, majestically
Portamento (Used in singing); the voice to be carried very smoothly
  from one note to the other
Quasi As if, almost
Risoluto Determined, resolutely

Scherzando, Scherzoso Playfully, piquantly, humorously
Sempre Always, throughout the movement or section
Senza Without
Soave, Suave Sweetly, flowingly
Sostenuto Sustained
Sotto voce In an undertone
Staccato Short, detached
Strepitoso Loudly, boisterously
Tacet Indicates that the part so marked has nothing to play during the
whole movement or passage
Tanto So much; *Allegro non tanto* Not so fast
Tenuta, Tenuto, Tenute, Ten. Held on, sustained
Tranquillo, Tranquillamente Quietly, calmly
Troppo Too much; *Allegro ma non troppo* Not too quickly
Volti subito, V.S. Turn over the page quickly

4 Intensity

Crescendo (cresc.) Becoming louder
Descrescendo (decresc.), Diminuendo (dim.) Becoming softer
Forte (f) Loud
Fortissimo (ff) Very loud
Mezzo forte (mf) Moderately loud
Mezzo piano (mp) Moderately soft
Piano (p) Soft
Pianissimo (pp) Very soft
Forte-piano (fp) Indicates a short forceful accent
Calando Gradually becoming softer and slower
Mancando
Morendo
Perdendosi } Dying away
Smorzando
Sforzando, Forzato Similar to fp

5 Instrumental terms

a Pianoforte

Una corda 'One string', i.e. use the left pedal
Tre corde Release (take up) the left pedal
Pedale or *Ped.* Use the right-hand (damper) pedal
M.D. (Mano destra) Use the right hand

> M.G. (*Main gauche*, Fr.) ⎫
> M.S. (*Mano sinistra*, It.) ⎬ Use the left hand

b Strings

pizzicato (*pizz.*) Pluck the strings with the finger instead of using the bow
arco Use the bow again
con sordino (plural *sordini*) With mute
senza sordino Without mute
·*sul ponticello* With the bow near the bridge
col legno Play with the back (or wood) of the bow
sul G Play on the G string only
⊓ Down bow
V Up bow
divisi (*div.*) Used in orchestral parts to show that a passage which is not in unison should be divided between the players
unison (*unis.*) All players play the same part

c Woodwind and brass

a 2 Two players to play the same part (In most scores 1st and 2nd wind parts are written on one stave.)
1 or *I* The first player only (the term *divisi* is peculiar to string parts)
2 or *II* The second player only
solo Alone (often with no or little accompaniment and therefore prominent)
sordino (*sord.*) Muted
senza sordino Without mute
tremolo (*trem.*) The rapid alternation of two notes. Similar to a trill but at an interval wider than a tone
flatterzunge (*flz.*) Flutter-tongue, i.e. play with a rolling tongue as for an 'r'
bouché (French) *gestopft* (German) A stopped or brassy note on the horn produced with the right hand pressed into the bell. Indicated with the sign +
naturale (*nat.*) Used as a contradiction of an unusual mode of playing and sometimes shown with the sign ○ after a stopped note

d Guitar

Pulgar (p) (Spanish) Thumb (of right hand)
Indice (i) (Spanish) Index finger
Medio (m) (Spanish) Middle finger
Annular (a) (Spanish) Ring finger
Barré (French), *Ceja* (Spanish) Bar (with the index finger of the right hand, stopping a number of strings at the same fret)
6e en re Tune the sixth string to D (a tone lower than the normal E)

Rasgueado (Rasg.) Brush stroke (fingertips brushed across strings)
Tambor (Tam.) Drum stroke (with fingertip, nail, or knuckle on strings near
  bridge or fret board or on wooden body of instrument)

6 Some French terms used in music

Animé With animation
Assez Enough or fairly (as in *assez vite* − fairly lively)
Bien Very
Cedez Slow down (equivalent to Italian *rallentando*)
Décidé With decision
Douce (Doux) Sweet
Emporté Carried away (excitedly)
Lugubre Dreary, lugubrious
Modéré Moderate in speed
Moins Less
Peu Little (*peu a peu* − little by little, i.e. gradually)
Plus More
Presque Almost
Rageur Ill-tempered
Retenu Hold back (equivalent to Italian *ritenuto*)
Revenir Return
Rhythmé Rhythmic
Sans Without
Serrez Press on (get quicker)
Sous Under
Soutenu Sustained
Très Very
Vif Lively

7 Some German terms used in music

Aber But
Bewegt, Beweglich With movement
Breit Broadly
Einfach Simply
Gehalten Sustained
Immer Always, throughout
Langsam Slowly
Lebhaft Lively
Mässig Moderately
Noch Still more

Rasch Quickly
Ruhig Calmly
Schnell Quickly
Sehr Very
Stark Loudly, Forcibly
Wenig A little, rather
Ziemlich Rather, moderately

II Melody and Harmony

NOTE: The harmonic system described in the next three chapters was used in Western music during the period c. 1650 – c. 1850. The modal harmony of the Renaissance period, the chromatic harmony introduced during the 19th century, and the various 20th-century harmonic systems devised by individuals or by 'schools' of composers all lie outside the scope of this book: further information on these may be found in specialized publications.

A The harmonic series

1   In most Western music of the last 400 years, melody and harmony are closely linked. The harmonic base influences the melodic shape, while the melody in turn implies certain harmonic progressions. These are influenced by the natural acoustical phenomenon known as the **harmonic series**.

2   Whenever a naturally-produced note is sounded, it not only vibrates at its fundamental pitch, but also, in variable but mostly diminishing strength, it vibrates at higher pitches. These vibrations are called **partials, overtones,** or **harmonics**.

3   Some of these can be heard clearly, but others are very faint. They arise because the strings, pipes, or vocal chords, which make the sound, are able to vibrate along their entire length, and also for half, a third, a quarter, fifth, sixth, and so on of their length.

4   This is the harmonic series produced by the fundamental note C.

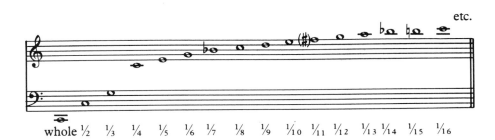

5 Notice that the intervals of the harmonic series get smaller as they rise.

6 When the notes equivalent to the first six harmonics are played together as a **chord**, they produce a familiar sound:

This natural phenomenon arises from any note. It forms the basis of our Western harmonic language.

B Triads

1 Two notes in this six-part chord derived from the harmonic series appear more than once. The essence of the chord is a triad, consisting of three different notes.

These three notes are the tonic, mediant and dominant in the key of C major.

2 A triad consists of a **root**, a **third**, and a **fifth**. It takes its name from its lowest note, or root, or from the degree of the scale on which it is formed.

3 Triads can be built on any degree of the scale, but those based on the tonic and dominant have had the greatest influence on harmonic development.

Key of C major

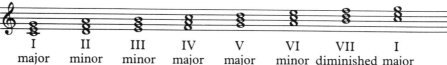

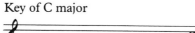

4   In a major scale, the triads on I, IV and V are all major triads, because the third
    above their root is a **major third**. The others are all minor triads, because the
    third above their root is a **minor third**, with the exception of chord VII, which is
    made up of two minor thirds, and is therefore a diminished triad.

5   The above triads are all said to be in **close position**. The notes of a triad may also
    be spaced out in **open position**:

e.g.

I   V

or doubled,
e.g.

I   V

C The dominant seventh

1   An additional note is often added to the triad on the dominant chord (e.g. G in
    the key of C).

2   This additional note is a minor 3rd above the fifth of the triad.

V   minor 3rd

3   As it is also a minor 7th above the root of the dominant triad, it is known as a
    dominant 7th.

   minor 7th

V7

Remember that this additional note, although a seventh in the chord, is *not* the
seventh degree of the scale, but the fourth, because it is reckoned from the
dominant.

4 The quality and function of the dominant 7th chord is influenced by the fact that it contains a tritone (or diminished 5th) which occurs between the third and seventh of the chord.

 diminished 5th or tritone

As we saw under Intervals (I L) the tritone is unstable. In a dominant 7th it tends to pull inwards towards the notes of the tonic chord.

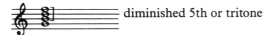

Play and write dominant 7ths in a number of major keys. Any triad can be changed into a 7th chord by adding an extra third, but in most music the dominant 7th appears far more often than other 7th chords.

D Chord Tunes

1 The individual notes of a chord, played or sung one at a time, produce a melodic unit or motif:

2 Add a rhythm and the motif comes to life:

3 Repeat it or extend it and it becomes a **phrase**:

4 In the absence of words, tempo, phrase and other marks establish its mood.

5 A number of well-known tunes are based on just one chord.

Come to the cook-house door boys, Come to the cook-house door

Notice the rhythmic and melodic repetition and the phrase structure: two similar phrases (A and A1), each lasting 2 bars, the first ending on the dominant, the second on the tonic.

With this as a model, write tunes in C and other keys.

Chord basis   I | I | I | I ‖

Phrase structure A | | A1 | ‖

6

There were ten in the bed And the lit-tle one said,'Roll o-ver. Roll o-ver.'

Here are two different two-bar phrases (A and B). The second complements the first, and each has a repeated motif.

Taking this as a model, write similar four-bar tunes in other keys.

Chord basis   I | I | I | I ‖

Phrase structure A | (A) | B | (B) ‖

7 Longer tunes are based on two or more chords.

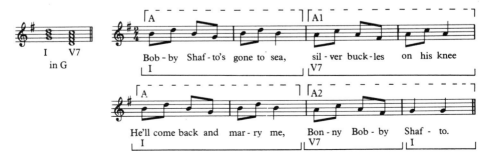

Bob - by Shaf - to's gone to sea, sil - ver buck - les on his knee

He'll come back and mar - ry me, Bon - ny Bob - by Shaf - to.

Notice the underlying chord pattern with its alternation of tonic and dominant 7th.

Notice the more rapid chord changes towards the end.

In this longer tune there are four similar phrases (A, A1, A, A2), of which the last ends on the tonic.

Use this as a model for other tunes.

Chord basis | I | I | V | V | I | I | V | I ‖

Phrase structure |A | | A1| | A | | A2| ‖

8   Or, a complementary second or fourth phrase could be written over the same chord basis.

Chord basis | I | I | V | V | I | I | V | I‖

Phrase structure |A | | B | | A | | B1 | ‖

9   Using the same chord basis, Mozart wrote this:

Mozart: *Piano Concerto in E flat, K482* (3rd movement)

Here the phrase structure is more subtle, with two two-bar phrases being complemented by a four-bar phrase which grows out of the same material. Notice the contour of the melody which rises, a phrase at a time, to bar 6, where a contrasting motif is introduced and then immediately repeated over a different chord.

Chord basis   I | I | V | V | I | I | V | I ‖

Phrase structure   A | | A1 | | A2 | B | (B) | ‖

Notice also that no phrase ends on the tonic until the end of the tune.

10   This natural progression, or drive, back towards a point of rest is assisted by certain underlying chord patterns, which tend to change more quickly towards the end. This is a form of punctuation and in music is known as a **cadence**.

The cadence formed by the chords V – I is called a **full** or **perfect cadence**, and acts like a full stop.

Cadences which end on V have the effect of a comma, and are known as **half** or **imperfect cadences**.

A fuller discussion of cadences in the context of four-part harmony may be found in IV F and G.

Chord tunes can be simply accompanied by playing the appropriate chord (I or V7 in these examples), under the melody in any convenient instrumental or vocal layout. Such instant 'do it yourself' harmonization will allow a ready appreciation of the harmonic effect, but will lack the refinement of a more careful choice of chord positions. (See Chapters III and IV.)

Look for other two-chord passages and also for other examples of 2 + 2 + 4-bar phrase structure which may or may not have the same chord basis.

E Non-chord notes and decorations

1   For greater variety, chord tunes may be decorated or embellished with non-chord notes.

2   Non-chord notes are of three kinds: **passing, leaning**, or **neighbouring**.
In theory they are termed **unessential**, as opposed to chord notes, which are classified as **essential**. In practice, however, they play a significant role in the expressive function of the melodic line.

3   **Passing notes** move by step between two chord notes.

Michael Finnigan

In bars 2 and 6 the note A links the chord notes B and G. In bar 4 the note E fills in a step in the chord of D. In each case the passing note creates a slight tension with the underlying harmony and pushes the melody forward.

Add passing notes to previous chord tunes, dividing the beat to accommodate the extra note.

Alternatively, write a new tune on the 'Michael Finnigan' pattern which has the same chord base and phrase structure as that in D8.

4 In the next example, the stepwise movement of the passing notes is contrasted with the arpeggios in the first two bars.

Bach: *Brandenburg Concerto No. 4 (Opening)*

In bars 2, 5 and 6 the note A is a chord note, but in bars 3 and 4 it is a passing note over the chord of G.

5 Passing notes are sometimes used in pairs, especially between the fifth of a chord and the root above, where the interval is a 4th instead of the more usual 3rd.

Handel: *Messiah*

In this example, the first passing note (B) falls on the beat, which gives it more urgency.

6 Passing notes which fall on the beat are called **accented passing notes**. They are a special form of **appoggiatura**, or leaning note.

7 A leaning note, or **appoggiatura** (from Italian *appoggiare*, to lean, or prop up) leans on a chord note and delays its appearance in the bar. It is always emphasized, and may last longer than the note it displaces. It need not be approached stepwise, as with an accented passing note, but usually moves on by step.

8 The appoggiatura is a feature of much Austrian music, especially waltz tunes. Here it seems to give the necessary lift and lilt to the music.

Johann Strauss II: *An der schönen blauen Donau (No. 2)*

Notice the extended chord base, one chord per phrase until the last, when there are five chord changes. Notice also the contours, the second phrase pitched higher and the third leading to a climax at the start of the fourth. The appoggiaturas (F sharp in bars 3 and 11, and E in bar 7) lean for four beats before arriving at their chord note.

9 During the 18th century appoggiaturas and accented passing notes were sometimes written in small notation to distinguish them from chord notes.

Haydn: *Piano Sonata No. 7, Hob XVII/D1* (2nd movement, Minuet)

This practice was a great help to the **continuo player** (see III B8) who filled in the harmonies from a figured bass.

10 Neighbouring notes or auxiliary notes are, as their name suggests, non-chord notes which are adjacent to a chord note. However, instead of passing on to another note, they return to the same note.

11 Neighbouring notes occur on or off the beat.

12 Neighbouring notes either occur one step above:

Ach, du lieber Augustin

13 Or one step below. In this case the step is sometimes adjusted to make it a semitone.

Alouette

Brahms: *Symphony No. 2* (1st movement, bar 44)

Use *Ach, du lieber Augustin* as a chord/phrase structure for a tune with upper and lower neighbouring notes.

14 Upper and lower neighbouring notes are sometimes used successively as a decoration of the same note and thereby form what is called a **turn**. Mozart's first presentation of the Concerto theme quoted at D 2 is decorated in this way. Compare this with the previous quotation.

Mozart: *Concerto in E flat, K482* (3rd movement, bar 1)

15 In this famous Weber tune the pattern is reversed to form an **inverted turn**:

Weber: *Der Freischütz* (Overture)

I   V7
in C

16 A pair of neighbouring notes is sometimes found decorating either side of a single chord note:

 or

or of a pair of chord notes a third apart, in which case they are termed **changing notes** or *note cambiate* (Italian).

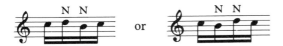

17 Sequence

If we look back at the Brandenburg Concerto (**E** 4), we will see that the motifs in bars 3 and 4 are repeated, one note lower, in bars 5 and 6. This is called a **sequence**.

A sequence is the immediate repetition of a motif or phrase at a higher or lower pitch. It is a useful way of extending a melody, since it uses the same idea to vary the sound. The repetition of a phrase one or more notes higher can raise the emotional temperature of the piece.

'Bobby Shafto' and the Mozart Concerto each contain brief sequences. Look at these examples again, then select, or make up, a chord/phrase structure and write a tune which includes a motif or phrase in sequence.

NB Without accidentals the semitone/tone arrangement will not be identical – this is called a tonal sequence. A 'real' sequence has identical intervals.

Here are two chord/phrase structures taken from Strauss waltzes which may be used as a basis for your own waltz melodies. Try to include appoggiaturas and sequences.

a *Lagunen-Waltzer, No. 1*

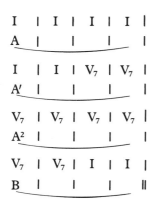

```
I  |  I  |  I  |  I  |
A  |     |     |     |

I  |  I  |  V₇ |  V₇ |
A' |     |     |     |

V₇ |  V₇ |  V₇ |  V₇ |
A² |     |     |     |

V₇ |  V₇ |  I  |  I  |
B  |     |     |     ‖
```

b *Morgenblätter, No. 5*

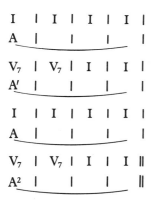

```
I  |  I  |  I  |  I  |
A  |     |     |     |

V₇ |  V₇ |  I  |  I  |
A' |     |     |     |

I  |  I  |  I  |  I  |
A  |     |     |     |

V₇ |  V₇ |  I  |  I ‖
A² |     |     |    ‖
```

Annotated examples for II B to E

Bach: *Brandenburg Concerto No. 2 in F* (1st movement)

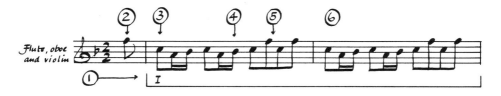

1 Chord basis – derived from Bach's lively running and jumping bass.
   Note varied rate of harmonic change. First and third lines, one chord only.
2 Anacrusis. Up-beat start found at the beginning of most sections throughout the movement.
3 First motif – stepwise with lively rhythm.
4 Passing note B flat between notes of the F chord.
5 Second motif – jumping.
6 First bar repeated to make a two-bar phrase.
7 Third motif – flowing.
8 Appoggiatura B flat leans on to the A of chord I.
9 Third bar repeated – balances first two-bar phrase. Leads downward at end.
10 First motif turned upside-down (inverted).
11 Modification of second motif.
12 Part of third motif.
13 Previous bar repeated with changed end.
14 Half-bar repeat increases excitement and leads towards climax.
15 Different chord as approach to perfect cadence (see II G). Coincides with climax of section.

Beethoven: *Piano Concerto No. 2* (1st movement)

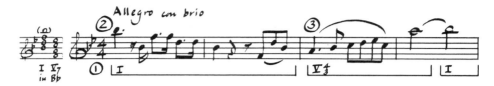

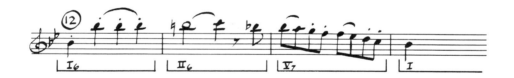

1   Chord basis. Arabic numerals refer to the inversions of the chords (see III B) used by Beethoven.

2   Opening statement on tonic chord.

3   Complementary flowing phrase over dominant/tonic harmony.

4   Answering statement on dominant chord.

5   Complementary phrase over tonic chord.

6   New lyrical phrase.

7   Chord II (supertonic) as approach to V (see II G).

8   Long appoggiatura rising to chord note (C) by a semitone.

9   Appoggiatura B flat leaning on chord note A.

10   Chromatic passing note.

11   Another semitone-rising appoggiatura over tonic chord.

12   Repeated phrase an octave higher with downward-moving ending.

F Shaping a melody

Choose a chord basis which moves away from and then back to the tonic, just like an outward and return journey.

I ——— V (and back to) ———I

Decide on a possible phrase structure.

A   A
A   B
A   A   A   A
A   A   A   B
A   A   B   A
A   B   B   A
A   B   A
A   B   A   B
A   B   A   C

Of course, both chord basis and phrase structure may change in the light of the subsequent motivic and melodic development.

Think up a short motif with a recognizable rhythmic and/or melodic identity. It might move by step (**conjunct motion**),

or leap (**disjunct motion**),

or include a repeated note figure with a definite pattern,

or have elements of all three.

Extend the motif into a phrase by repetition,

by sequence,

by inversion, which involves turning the pattern upside-down without necessarily reproducing the intervals exactly,

or by the addition of a balancing motif.

Aim for a distinct shape or contour, rather than a melody which hops up and down at random.

Make sure the tune is singable or suitable for the instrument for which it is written.

Phrases are usually two or four bars long, but may be compressed or stretched for greater variety or expressive purposes. When this happens it is necessary to consider the length of the other phrases in the melody. Should any be the same or should they compensate by being longer or shorter?

Complete the structure with answering, or complementary, phrases. Take care to avoid a feeling of finality until the end by adjusting the melody, where necessary, to avoid the tonic on any strong beats at the end of phrases. Consider the overall unity of the melody when developing B and C tunes. They should give variety as well as balancing and belonging. Many extended melodies are entirely developed from one original motif.

Lead towards a climax. This is often most effective when reached in or towards the last phrase.

The shape and mood of a melody may be clarified by adding indications of tempo, dynamics and articulation.

Compare the following examples, both of which have identical notes:

Now look again at the annotated example of the Bach Brandenburg Concerto and, in particular, at the development of the three motifs and the overall contour as well as the placing of the climax.

G Approach chords

1 Two chords embellished with a few non-chord notes allow considerable melodic invention. But unrelieved two-chord passages can become boring.

2 The insertion of a new chord on the approach to V gives thrust and forward direction to the phrase.

3 There are numerous approach chords to V, of which the most commonly used (or implied) is the chord of II.

II in its diatonic form is a minor triad (which gives additional variety).

NB It is frequently found as a first inversion (see III B1) and in an altered chromatic form as a major or diminished chord (see Chapter IV).
And it is significant that just as V is a fourth below I,

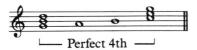

so II is a fourth below V,

and it is this which seems to give it its strength and suitability as an approach chord.

4   As with the dominant triad, the supertonic chord of II is often used with an added 7th:

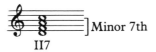

II7   ] Minor 7th

The 7th pulls downward and this gives even greater movement towards V.

II7   V

5   The top three notes of the supertonic 7th are identical with the major triad on the subdominant,

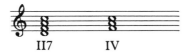

II7   IV

and in some music this chord is favoured as an approach to V.

Use any instrument or group of voices to become familiar with the sound of these chords.

Using convenient instrumental positions, play the progression below with one chord per bar:

    I   I   II($_7$)   V
    I   II($_7$)   V   I

In the key of C the bass notes will be as follows:

Work out the progression in a number of other keys.

Annotated examples for F and G

Early One Morning

1 First four-bar phrase. Largely broken-chord (disjunct) movement.
2 Supertonic chord. The last note of the bar may be thought of either as a passing note or as the seventh of the supertonic chord.
3 First phrase repeated with changed ending leading to a perfect cadence.
4 Shorter phrase (two bars) with smoother motion – repeated.
5 Climax phrase derived from previous broken chord and scalewise ideas.
6 Appoggiaturas (or accented passing notes). E and C leaning on D and B flat of supertonic chord.
7 Similar appoggiaturas. A and F leaning on notes of dominant chord.

Haydn: *'Clock' Symphony* No. 101 (2nd movement)

1 Pizzicato harmonic accompaniment.
2 Leaping motif, complemented with a scale figure and in bar 4 a dotted-note idea.
3 Harmony remains on tonic chord.
4 Quicker chord change towards imperfect (half) cadence.
5 Supertonic chord as approach to V. Haydn slips in a C sharp in the bass on the last quaver which leads even more strongly towards the dominant chord.
6 Repeat of melodic material.
7 Scale figure extended and raised to a climax.
8 Chord II as approach to perfect (full) cadence.
9 Haydn's E in the melody is ninth above the dominant, and therefore (strictly) forms a chord of V_9.

H Melodies in minor keys and modes

1 Melodies in minor keys and modes work on the same principles as those in major keys.

2 Major and minor keys exchange chords fairly freely so that the triad on a particular degree may occur in a different form (e.g. minor instead of diminished, or major instead of minor).

   The most common example of this is the use of a *major* chord on the dominant of a *minor* key.

D minor

I   V

Here the middle note of V is raised to form a true leading note in the harmonic minor scale of D, and consequently forms a chord of A major rather than A minor.

3 As a result of this modification to chord V, the interval between the sixth and seventh degrees of the minor scale becomes an augmented 2nd (see the discussion on page 47). The augmented 2nd has a characteristic sound and is difficult to pitch, so unless a special melodic effect is required it is usual to raise the sixth degree as well, to smooth out the melody.

D minor

4 Where the chord of V is *not* implied, the leading note is not necessarily raised, which means that a chromatic adjustment to the sixth degree is *not* required.

D minor

5 Melodic minor scales show the sixth and seventh raised in the ascending form, and both degrees restored to their original position in the descending. Many tunes feature this natural tendency, but where the harmonic basis is strong the practice outlined in 3 and 4 above is adopted.

6 Modal melodies are often associated with folk-songs.
   Modal melodies which have a clear chordal structure often imply a chord other than I or V in a primary, rather than purely approach role.

What shall we do with the drunken sailor?

Chorus from *Old Joe Clarke*

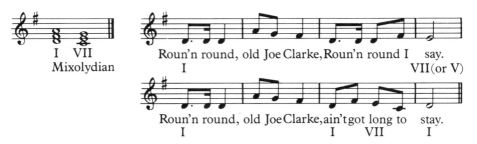

I   VII

Mixolydian   I

Roun'n round, old Joe Clarke, Roun'n round I   say.

VII (or V)

Roun'n round, old Joe Clarke, ain't got long to   stay.

I   I   VII   I

In both the above melodies this chord is on the seventh degree.

In a major key, VII is diminished and rarely occurs other than as a first inversion (see III B2).

In a modal context, VII is either a minor or major triad, which gives it structural stability.

7   In a major scale, the tritone occurs between the fourth and seventh notes of the scale. But in the modes, with the exception of the Lydian mode, it occurs between other degrees,
e.g. in the Dorian between III and VI

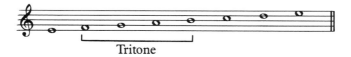

Tritone

and in the Phrygian between II and V.

Tritone

In modal melodies, the interval of the tritone is usually avoided as it does not lead towards the tonic (chord) as it does in the major scale.

I   Modulation and melodic structure

1   Most folk-songs and other simple tunes remain in one key throughout.

2   When a melody or piece of music does move from one key to another it is said to **modulate**.

3   The most common modulations are to closely related keys.

   Major key melodies may move to the *dominant* key,
and sometimes to the *relative minor* key,
and to the *subdominant* key,
e.g. from the key of G, to D, E minor, or C.

   Minor key melodies may move to the *relative major*,
and sometimes to the *subdominant minor*,
or the *dominant minor*,
e.g. from the key of G minor, to B flat major, C minor or D minor.
   In addition, modulation between the tonic major and minor is sometimes found, e.g. G major to G minor, or G minor to G major.

4   It is usual to return to the tonic key at the end of a melody or piece.

5   A modulation is established by a perfect cadence in the new key. To make the transition from the old key to the new key as smooth as possible, the perfect cadence in the new key may be preceded by a chord common to both keys. This is known as a *pivot chord*: e.g. from C major to G major, a good pivot chord would be VI in C major (= II in G major), if the melody allows. Chord II in the new key is often used as a pivot chord, but others are also possible.

6   In a single melody line (i.e. without underlying harmonies) a modulation to a related key would be difficult, or even impossible, to spot straight away. If the third of the dominant chord in the new key is not used, there may well be no accidental to indicate a change of key. In this case, the modulation is said to be *implied*.

7   A melody may modulate at any point, but most often at the end of a phrase. Examples of modulation to the dominant are common at the end of the first half of a tune, and to the dominant or relative minor in the third phrase of an A A B A structure.
   Subdominant modulations are usually touched on in the second half. Some minor tunes fluctuate between the minor and the relative major from phrase to phrase.
   Study the annotated examples and then write melodies of similar structure. It helps to write out the chords of V and I in both the original and new keys before starting the melody.

Annotated examples for I

The Blue Bells of Scotland

1   II in the new key of A major.
2   V in the new key of A major. G sharp is the third of the dominant chord in that key.
3   Modulation to the dominant confirmed at the end of the third phrase. (Note that the first line is *repeated*, making two identical phrases.)
4   Immediate return to the tonic key.

The Vicar of Bray

1   V and I, or perfect cadence, in tonic key of D.

2   At end of third phrase, modulation to dominant implied. The note B (the fifth of the dominant chord in A) being followed by the tonic in that key suggests a perfect cadence in A major.

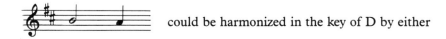 could be harmonized in the key of D by either

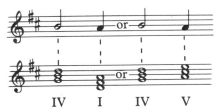

But in this part of the tune, immediately before the last phrase, neither alternative has the strength of the modulation to the dominant.

Schubert: *Symphony No. 2* (3rd movement: Trio)

1   Appoggiatura E flat leans on note of B flat chord (V_7 in E flat).
     (This note may also be considered as a *suspension* as it is preceded in the previous bar by the same note as part of the harmony. See Chapter IV, J).
2   Perfect cadence at end of phrase in the dominant key, i.e. B flat major. C is part of V in B flat and the note B flat is the tonic. Notice that the qualifying A natural does not occur in the melody but forms part of the V_7 chord.
3   Immediate return to tonic key of E flat.
4   Appoggiatura (suspension) A flat on to G of E flat chord (I in key of E flat).
5   Treated as a sequence, now the appoggiatura leans on D of B flat chord (V_7 in E flat).
6   Modulation to dominant (V_7 – I in key of B flat).
7   Again an immediate return to tonic key of E flat and to first idea.
8   An approach to the perfect cadence in tonic key of E flat through the chord of A flat, which is the subdominant. Compare bar 6, which leads towards the dominant key at the end of the first phrase.
9   Perfect cadence in tonic key.

Bach: *Minuet* from the *Anna Magdalena Notebook* (BWV Anh. 132)

1   Start of modulation to relative major.
2   Confirmed with perfect cadence in F major.
3   Continuation in F major.
4   Sequence back in D minor.
5   Melodic minor scale over chord of V in D minor.
6   II as approach to V.
7   Perfect cadence in original tonic – D minor.

J Word setting

1 When setting words, the music should enhance, but not distort, the natural speech-rhythm and inflection of the voice.

2 The melody should reflect the **mood** of the words, as well as interpreting the speech-rhythm.
Approach the setting of a verse in the following way:

a Read through the lines, noting the stressed syllables and especially important words.

Old Meg she was a Gipsy,
And lived upon the moors;
Her bed it was the brown heath turf,
And her house was out of doors.

b Write the words under a stave and put a half bar-line in front of the accented words:

Old Meg she was a Gipsy, And lived upon the moors;

c Decide which time (duple, triple, quadruple; simple or compound) will best suit the words and lightly pencil in the rhythm with due regard to 1 above. The final choice of metre may be entirely dictated by mood – each of the following has some merit. Be sure each syllable has its own note.

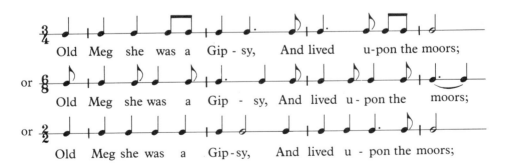

(Remember to complement any anacrusis with the correct number of beats at the end of the tune.)

d Next, convert the rhythmic sketch into a melody, which should take account of the guides offered under Section F of this chapter. Take care to make it suitable for singing, and in general avoid excessive leaps, especially those which continue to leap in the same direction (unless you wish to emphasize a particular word, such as 'jump'). Do not exceed the normal range of a particular voice.

Old   Meg she was   a   Gip - sy,   And lived u-pon the   moors;   Her

bed   it was the brown heath turf, And her house was out of   doors.

e Now decide whether any words might benefit from more than a single sound, or be emphasized in other ways.

Perhaps the second half could be improved by the following changes:

Her bed it was the   brown heath turf, And her house   was out of   doors.

Here 'brown' is given additional warmth and richness with a leaning note and the two sounds to a single syllable are slurred together accordingly. Where space permits, a line is added to the underlay (text) to show the continuation of the word.

In the penultimate bar, 'out' is given particular prominence by being lengthened. Note the change of time and the change back to ⁶⁄₈. This treatment, although irregular, does help to break what might otherwise become a rather tum-ti-tum setting. A similar effect could have been achieved with a pause, with no change of time.

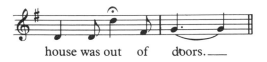

house was out   of   doors. ___

f Finally, add tempo and other expression marks. In a vocal part these are usually placed **above** the stave so that they are not confused with the words.

III Inversions and two-part writing

A Bass lines

1 Chords are presented as successions of vertical blocks only in very simple harmonizations. In the previous chapter, they were shown in this way in order to clarify the harmonic structure of the melodies.

2 In practice, chords are broken up into a variety of figurations and spacings:

or embellished with non-chord notes.

3 The lowest part or voice in a piece of music is called the **bass**. It has the lowest note of the chords, but need not necessarily be so low that it has to be written in the bass clef.

4 The bass is often as important as the melody. Many pieces, especially those for keyboard, are essentially in only two parts, a melody and a bass.

5 Harmony grows upwards from the bass, which plays an essential part in the identification of chords. It is said that a well-written piece should make sense with just the top and bottom parts.

Here Bach's bass steps firmly down the roots of I – V – I. Notice the use of a high and low G for the tonic chords. Compare the stepwise movement of the violins and violas with the held note of the first flute. Notice also the lighter texture in bars 4 and 5 (see Chapter V).

Bach: *Brandenberg Concerto No. 4* (1st movement)

6   A chord with its root in the lowest part is said to be in **root position**. Bass lines do not, however, only use the roots of chords. Chords may be rearranged into **inversions** so that a note other than the root is in the bass.

Schubert: *Symphony No. 2* (3rd movement: Trio)

Here in bar 2, Schubert rearranges, or *inverts*, the chord of the dominant 7th so that F comes in the bass instead of B flat, as occurs in the fourth bar. This gives a smoother, more melodic bass line. The violin part has a lively figuration built on broken chords or chordal skips.

B Inversions

1 Inversions can be formed from any chord, but, as with root positions, some occur more frequently than others. All the chords introduced in the last chapter are used in their first inversion, which has the third of the triad in the bass. The chord of II is much more common in this form.

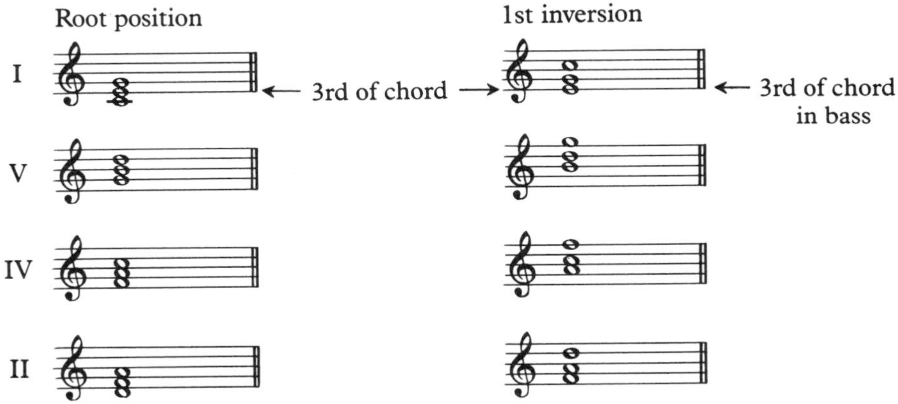
Root position
1st inversion
I
← 3rd of chord →
← 3rd of chord in bass
V
IV
II

2 In addition, chord VII occurs almost exclusively in its first inversion. VII is a diminished triad, built on the leading note, and it rarely appears in root position.

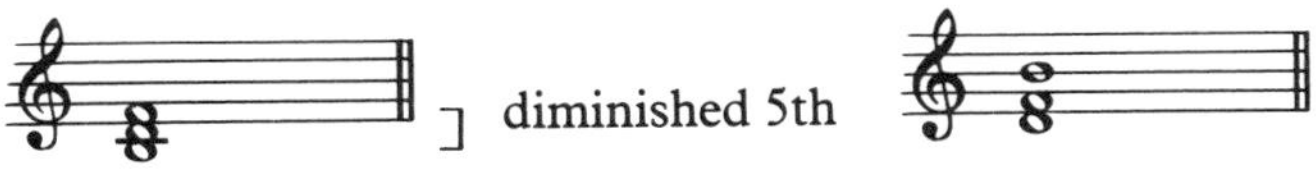
diminished 5th

In its first inversion it has many functions, including that of bridging the gap between the root position and first inversion of I.

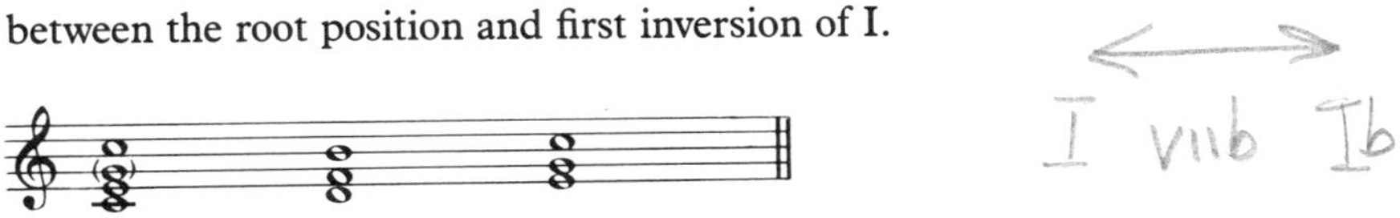
I viib Ib

3 As in root position, the notes of an inversion may be spaced out into an **open position**.

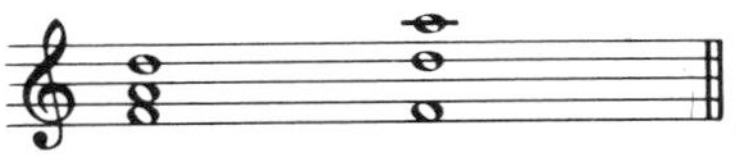

4 Root position chords are sometimes labelled $^5_3$. This figuring shows that the notes of the triad are a third and fifth above the root.

First inversions are accordingly labelled $^6_3$ or, more often, just 6. This shows that the notes of the chord are a third and sixth above the bass note (not the root which is now higher up).

First inversion chords are known also as Ib, IIb, etc.

5 Triads may be inverted a further time to produce **second inversions**, although in practice their appearance is much more restricted.

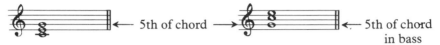

They occur most often at cadences and are closely linked to the next chord. In this situation they are sometimes called **cadential $^6_4$s**. The figuring shows that the notes are now a fourth and a sixth above the bass. (They are also referred to as Ic and IVc.) There are rarely cadential $^6_4$s on any other degrees of the scale.

The cadential $^6_4$ is best thought of as a pair of appoggiaturas embellishing the next chord.

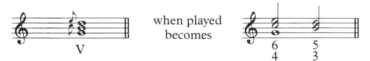

when played becomes

The $^6_4$ always occurs on a stronger beat than the following chord.

6 Second inversions occasionally have other functions:

a As **passing chords** bridging the gap (as did VII$_6$) between the root position and first inversion of another chord:

b As **arpeggio chords**, in association with the root position and first inversion of the *same* chord:

c And as **alternating chords**. Some bass lines, especially in march tunes, alternate between root position and second inversion of the same chord:

These functions are seldom found in two-part writing and are dealt with more completely in **IV D 9-12**.

7 Because they are made up of four notes, 7th chords, like dominant 7ths, can be inverted yet again:

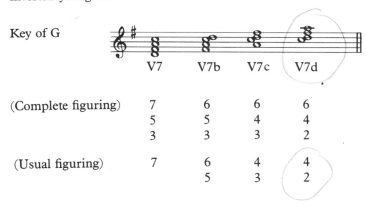

Key of G

	V7	V7b	V7c	V7d
(Complete figuring)	7	6	6	6
	5	5	4	4
	3	3	3	2
(Usual figuring)	7	6	4	4
		5	3	2

Examples of third inversions are readily found in two-part writing, where they are distinguished by the interval of a major 2nd or sometimes by an augmented 4th. The seventh of the chord comes in the bass and falls to the third of the tonic chord.

8 In the 17th and 18th centuries composers sometimes wrote down only the melody and bass parts, leaving the **continuo player** to fill in the harmonies on a keyboard instrument or other instrument capable of playing chords. In most instances, two notes (top and bottom) were sufficient to fix the harmony, but, in order to help the player, figures were sometimes added beneath the bass line;

hence the term **figured bass**. Any note in the harmony which needed to be raised or lowered was shown with an accidental alongside, or in place of, the figures.

Bach: Trio Sonata from *The Musical Offering* (Allegro)

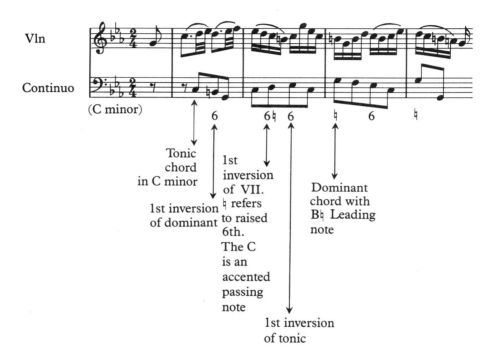

9   Inversions allow greater variety and flow in the bass line, which would otherwise have to leap from root to root. They also provide a valuable alternative to root positions, since they are less stable and strong.

Second inversions are always used in association with adjacent chords. They never occur in independent positions, and should be used only when their function is understood.

Annotated examples for B

Mozart: *Duo, K496a*

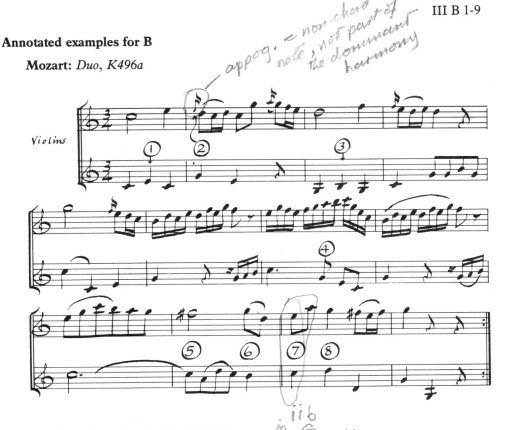

Violins

1 First inversion of tonic chord of C between two root positions.
2 Appoggiatura E written in 18th-century style, showing clearly that the first note of group is a non-chord note and is not part of the dominant harmony.
3 First inversion of dominant 7th, between two root positions.
4 Second inversion as part of an arpeggio bass line down the tonic chord.
5 Modulation to dominant key of G. F sharp in first violin forms, with second violin notes, a chord of V7 in G. The note C at end of group forms a chord of V7d which moves on to
6 First inversion of G chord.
7 II$_6$ in key of G.
8 Ic as a cadential $^6_4$, moving immediately to V in key of G as part of perfect cadence. The second beat, on which the $^6_4$ chord occurs, is stronger than the third.

Bach: *Minuet* from the *Anna Magdalena Notebook* (BWV Anh. 132)

1 Bass line mixes stepwise passages with stronger leaps which mainly occur near the cadences.
2 VII$_6$ (the D in melody is an appoggiatura). Full chord would be E – (G) – C sharp.
3 I$_6$, tonic chord of D minor in first inversion.
4 II$_6$ or, as it is unqualified with a third note, could be IV. II$_6$ is more characteristic of Bach's approach to V.
5 Moving towards F major (relative major of D minor).
6 I$_6$ in F major.
7 Perfect cadence in F major.

8   Linking figure which leads back to bar 1 and is then imitated by the right hand. Such interplay between parts gives greater vitality and unity to the two-part writing.

9   Standard tonic – dominant – tonic movement in chordal skips under last note.

10 Continuation in F major with two-bar phrase.

11 I_6 in F.

12 II_6 in F.

13 V_4^6 as arpeggio.

14 Sequential imitation in D minor of previous two-bar phrase.

15 Moving quavers which run into

16 Right hand, which imitates and then takes them to a

17 Climax in the penultimate bar.

18 II_6 as approach to perfect cadence in D minor.

C Two-part writing

1   Look again at the previous examples of two-part writing. Notice that each part has an interesting melodic line. Indeed, the parts almost have a conversation with each other; in the Mozart by adding comments here and there, and in the Bach by passing ideas from one to the other.

2   To write well in two parts it is necessary to have a clear phrase structure and chord framework in mind. Details may be changed as ideas grow out of the melodic parts.

3   Inversions and root positions will help to make a lively bass line, and the elaboration of the basic harmony with passing and neighbouring notes will help the music to flow.

4   Let the parts have some rhythmic independence by not writing note against note throughout.

5   Never let the two parts run along together in parallel unisons, octaves, or even perfect fifths. The result of this would be, effectively, to reduce the music to a single part.

Octaves   Perfect 5ths   unisons

6 Parallel 3rds and 6ths sound well, provided they do not go on for too long. Three or four in succession are usually enough.

7 Movement by **contrary motion** allows the greatest independence between the parts while at the same time avoiding undesirable consecutive octaves and 5ths.

8 Single appearances of octaves and 5ths are usually satisfactory especially at the beginning and end, or on the dominant chord of a perfect cadence.

9 A single octave sounds well when it is approached and quitted by step in contrary motion.

10 And a perfect 5th between a 3rd and 6th forming part of the same chord gives a valuable contrast of interval within similar motion.

This progression is often referred to as a 'Horn call', because of its association with the notes produced by a pair of natural horns. See again the Schubert example at A6 in this chapter.

11 Occasional 7ths may occur as a result of independent melodic movement where one part remains still and the other moves through a passing note. Such brief clashes add life to the music but need to be treated with care.

12 Both parts may be written on a single stave with stems turned up and down or, alternatively, on two staves.

13 When writing or studying a two-part piece it is often helpful to list the available chords on each degree of the scale in the relevant key. At this stage they are:

the **primary triads**

Key of D

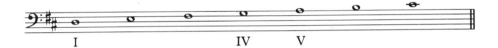

and their **inversions**,

plus **II and its 1st inversion** as approach chords,

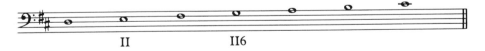

VII$_6$ as a link chord between I and I$_6$,

I $^6_4$ and **IV** $^6_4$ as cadential decorations of V $^5_3$ and I $^5_3$,

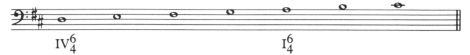

IV$^6_4$ I$^6_4$

and the **dominant 7th** with its inversions.

(In two-part writing, the last of these, with its downward pull to I$_6$, is the most useful.)

V$^4_2$ V7

Choice actually arises only on the second and fourth degrees, as, on the tonic and dominant, the $^6_4$ chords are always linked directly with their $^5_3$ resolution.

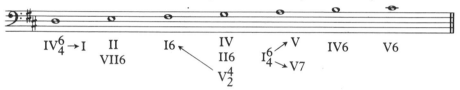

IV$^6_4$ →I   II   I6   IV   I$^6_4$ ↗V   IV6   V6
          VII6   II6   ↘V7
                           V$^4_2$

14   J. C. F. Bach (J. S. Bach's 16th child) uses just these chords in his two-part *Peasant Dance* in the key of D. It is set out here phrase by phrase:

bar 1

- *bar 1* Rhythmic chordal skipping figure over descending scale motif. The gap between the first inversion and root position of the tonic chord is filled with a passing note E. (As the tempo is lively, it can be assumed that, in all similar stepwise movement, the second quaver is a passing note.)
- *bar 2* Right hand takes up the scale motif in parallel 3rds (+ two octaves) with the left hand. As in bar 1, passing notes on second quaver between first inversion and root position, but in this bar, chord VII.
- *bar 3* Sequential treatment a note lower, accounting for a rather lengthy succession of parallel thirds. Chord I (or, allowing for the last bass note of bar, chord VI as a substitute – see IVc).

bar 4 Scale motif continued over dominant. Imperfect cadence at end of Phrase A.

bar 5 As bar 1.
bar 6 As bar 2.
bar 7 Contrary motion chordal skips leading to V on 3rd beat.
bar 8 Octave on tonic chord of perfect cadence at end of Phrase A¹. Chordal skips in left hand fill in beats in traditional pattern.

bar 9 Rhythmic pattern from bar 1 now used in ascending scale passage over dominant. (On the third quaver, the G in the lower part implies the last inversion of the dominant 7th moving on to I_6 in the next bar, although the passing note B in the upper part momentarily results in a chord of IV.)
bar 10 First inversion tonic chord with stepwise motif in contrary motion. Octave E on second quaver, between two positions of same chord.
bar 11 Move towards dominant with G sharp in left hand.
bar 12 Chord of A with semiquaver figure of bar 1 inverted melodically and placed on second beat rather than third. End of B phrase on, or in, dominant.

bar 13 Straight back on to tonic chord with bar 1 figure.
bar 14 Stepwise, but now in contrary motion rather than parallel thirds as in bar 2. Now supertonic chord II implied, there being no C sharp in this bar.

bar 15 Parallel sixth leading to perfect cadence through I₆, IV and V.
bar 16 Octave D. End of A² phrase. The entire structure is AABA, or **binary form** (see Chapter VI).

Annotated examples for III C

Handel: *Minuet in D minor*

1 Chordal skipping figures for the start of the phrase define tonic and dominant chords.
Notice the octaves at the beginning and end of each section and the alternation of root position and first inversion chords in bars 1, 2, 3, 5, 6 and so on.
2 Contrasting stepwise movement over subdominant chord.
3 Imperfect cadence on dominant.
4 Last inversion of dominant 7th with the C sharp and E from earlier in the bar completing the chordal effect. The 7th, G, moves down in the next bar to F.
5 Instead of being the third of a D minor chord, F is now the root of an F major chord.
The complementary second phrase starts with an idea based on the previous bar and continues in F major.
6 Three changes of harmony in bar before
7 The perfect cadence in F.
8 First phrase transposed from D minor into F major.

9 Fourth phrase straight back into D minor with material related to second phrase. Notice the perfect 5th on third quaver, between thirds, with the upper part moving by step.

10 Quicker change of harmony in penultimate bar. Second quaver implies $^6_4$ chord of D minor moving to $^5_3$ dominant chord on third quaver. Notice octave jump in bass which is characteristic of this cadential progression.

Mozart: *Minuet in D, K94*

1.   Rhythm of anacrusis ♩♪|♩ is repeated in subsequent phrases.
   Opening idea with regular harmonic pattern: two beats tonic, one beat dominant.
2.   Imitative entry in left hand which continues as a canon.
   Notice emphasis on contrary motion between hands.
3.   Short opening phrases now contrasted with long sweep of four bars.
4.   Moving into dominant key of A major through supertonic chord of B minor in new key.
5.   Dominant 7th chord in A, with appoggiatura A in right hand.
6.   Last inversion of A major dominant 7th, with E in right hand classed as a chord note, because it is quitted by leap.
   D is seventh of dominant 7th chord, falling to
7.   C sharp in left hand. Followed by $^6_4$ $^5_3$ on second and third beats with octave jump in lower part.
8.   New idea in middle section with rhythm derived from first phrase.
   Thicker three-part texture (see Chapter V). Mostly over dominant.
9.   Chromatic figure moving downwards in contrast to previous phrase. Again, mostly over dominant.
10.   Minor chord borrowed from tonic minor key.
11.   Return of first idea indicating ternary form (see Chapter VI).
12.   Characteristic large downward swoop in melody to initiate last phrase, which is modified to close in tonic.
13.   Perfect 5th above the bass note A with C sharp makes the first chord of the cadence.

IV Harmony in four parts

A Vocal harmony and voice-leading

1   Although many instrumental pieces are based on four-part harmony, this
    texture is more immediately associated with voices. Hymns are traditionally
    harmonized in four parts with a change of chord on each syllable of the text.
    For convenience, the parts for soprano, alto, tenor and bass (SATB) are set
    out on a treble and bass stave with stems turned *up* for soprano and tenor
    and *down* for alto and bass.

2   A working range for choral voices may be taken as:

> NB When, as in open score, each voice has its own stave, the tenor is usually
>   notated in the treble clef, with the convention that the voice will sound an
>   octave lower than written. To confirm this, an 8 is sometimes placed below
>   the clef.

3   To produce the best sound, the vertical spacing of the four voices should try to
    reflect the natural spacing of the harmonic series, with the largest space between
    bass and tenor.

This: 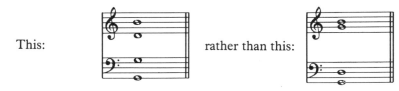 rather than this:

The *third* of the chord should not be placed too low in the tenor part:

This is more acceptable 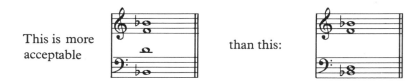 than this:

4 Apart from the vertical layout, the way in which each voice leads from one chord to the next must be considered.

The following points should be kept in mind:

a The **melody** (usually in the soprano) must be well-shaped and singable. It should not leap too much and, where it does, should return *within* the interval to the next sound.

This:  rather than this:

b The **bass** may, on occasions, move more boldly, especially by the leap of an octave, but again should return within the interval and be singable.

This:  not this:

c The **inside parts** (alto and tenor) will be more confined and therefore more restricted in their melodic movement. (This is particularly true of the *alto*.) Their function is to confirm the identity of the chords and to fill in the texture. They derive great strength from repeated notes, but at times have more melodic passages.

d In general, the three upper parts should aim to move to the nearest note of the next chord.

5 In addition, the following reminders and guides about the relationship of voices should be noted.

a As a rule, parts *should not cross*.

Except between

V and I in

Tenor and Bass

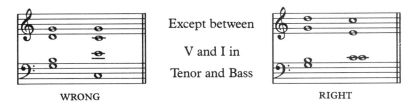

WRONG   RIGHT

b Nor should they overlap except between two positions of the same chord.

RIGHT   WRONG

c No two parts should move in unison, or in parallel octaves or fifths; con-figurations such as those given below should be avoided:

unisons between
alto and tenor

octaves between
bass and alto

fifths between
bass and tenor

d Further, between outside parts which sound more exposed, an octave or a fifth should not be approached by similar motion, unless the upper part moves by step. As with much voice-leading, the use of **contrary motion** overcomes such exposed fifths and octaves.

correct
(octave approached by
step in the upper voice)

weak and exposed
(fifth approached by
leap in the upper voice)

practical
(fifth approached
in contrary motion)

Where there is *no change* of harmony, exposed fifths and octaves become part of the total sonority, and therefore are no longer so prominent.

B Doubling

1   When writing in two parts it is sometimes difficult to define a chord, because one note of the triad is missing. In practice, this is rarely a problem, provided that the melody and bass together make good harmonic sense.

2   In four-part harmony, it is necessary to double one (or sometimes two) notes in order to expand the triad into a chord for four voices or instruments to play.

3   In major keys, the primary triads I, IV, and V are all major and sound best with either the *root* or *fifth* doubled. The third is not normally doubled in a major chord, since, by doing so, its harmonics (one of which clashes strongly with the harmonics of the other two notes) are unduly strengthened. Occasionally this vibrancy is exploited deliberately but is best avoided in early exercises.

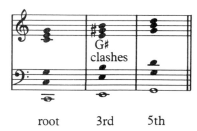

root   3rd   5th

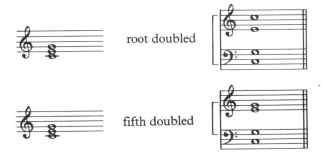

root doubled

fifth doubled

4   Sometimes the root is trebled and the fifth (but *not* the third) omitted.

root trebled

5   *Minor triads* sound well with either root, third or fifth doubled, since (in contrast with major triads) the harmonics arising from the third of a minor triad clash less violently.

6   Because the notes forming a tritone have a restricted progression towards the notes of the tonic chord, the root and fifth of a *diminished triad* are *not* doubled. In both root position (which is rare) and in first inversion it is best to double the *third*.

7   Never double the *leading note* in any chord, and rarely double a major third.

    Write out chords in four parts, doubling notes in ways suitable for major, minor, and diminished triads.

C Substitute and associate chords

1   In II G, we found that the chord of the supertonic is interchangeable with that of the sub-dominant in its function as an approach chord to the dominant. As in the relationship of the major to the relative minor key, the chord of II is a minor third lower than IV and is itself a minor triad.

2   In some harmonic progressions, the primary chord is replaced or associated with the chord on the root a minor third lower:

So I may be replaced by VI; V by III; IV by II.
But whereas examples of the use of II and VI are common, that of III is uncommon and often less satisfactory in effect.

3   Here are typical progressions showing the use of these chords.

   a VI in place of I (sometimes forming an Interrupted Cadence)

V   VI

VI in association with I linking it with IV

I   VI   IV   V

Notice the bass falling by thirds and the strong binding repeated note in the tenor.
The substitute chord of VI is rarely used in its first inversion.

   b III in place of or association with V

V   III   VI

III is rarely used in inversion.

c II in place of or association with IV

VI   IV   II   V

Again notice the bass falling by thirds and then strongly rising by a fourth to the dominant.

d II is as often used with an added 7th. When it resolves, the 7th moves down a step, usually to the leading note in the dominant chord.

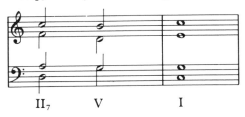

II₇   V   I

Both II and II₇ are used in their first inversions and occur far more frequently than the other two chords.

4   Similar substitutions are used in minor keys.

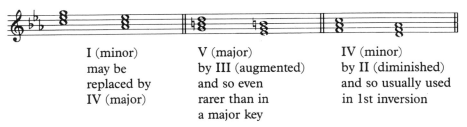

I (minor)	V (major)	IV (minor)
may be	by III (augmented)	by II (diminished)
replaced by	and so even	and so usually used
IV (major)	rarer than in	in 1st inversion
	a major key	

5 VII in its first inversion is sometimes used as a substitute for V. Other substitutions occur including those arising from the alternation of chords in their major and minor forms.

Annotated example for IV C

Victory (adapted from Palestrina)

1 Repeated tonic chords.
(Consecutive fifths and octaves not created when there is no onward movement to another chord.)
2 Repeated Ds in tenor part characteristic of inside parts, providing stability against melody and leaping bass.
3 A bar of minor substitute chords – III – II – VI.
Notice rate of chord change: bar 1, one chord; bar 2, two chords; and bar 3, three chords moving towards cadence.

4   Second phrase almost a sequence of first phrase a third lower.
5   Chords VI and III.
6   First phrase repeated with one unusual chord change.
7   Single example of a first inversion chord, in this context.

D Inversions in four parts

1   Any root position chord may be rearranged to form a first inversion or $\frac{6}{3}$ chord, although, in practice, appearances of III₆ or VI₆ are infrequent.

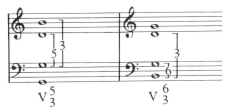

2   On the contrary, II and VII are most commonly found as first inversions.

3   As with root position chords, double the root (which is not now the bass), or fifth of **major** chords,

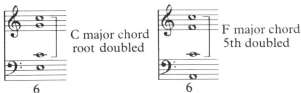

and double the root, third (now the bass) or fifth of **minor** chords,

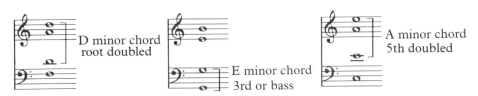

Double the third (or bass) *only* of **diminished** chords.

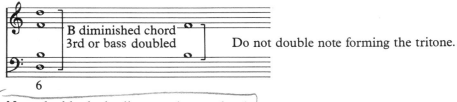

B diminished chord
3rd or bass doubled

Do not double note forming the tritone.

6

Never double the leading note in any chord.

4 Except for VII₆, all first inversion chords are weaker in effect than their equivalent root position chords.

5 Typical uses of primary chord inversions are:
a As an alternative in association with root position.

b As a neighbouring chord, with stepwise movement in the bass.

6 The first inversion of the supertonic is typically used as an approach to V,

but is also used on a weaker beat after the chord of IV.

7   VII₆ is typically found in the following contexts:
a As a **passing chord** between I and I₆

b Between IV and I

c And after V on a weaker beat.

8 A succession of first inversion chords is sometimes found in which the soprano moves in parallel sixths and the alto in parallel thirds with the bass. The tenor alternately doubles the fifth and the root of the chord.

9 Second inversion chords are *always* associated with their immediate neighbouring harmonies and *never* have an entirely independent existence.

As two of the notes are really the result of voice-leading (i.e. appoggiaturas or other unessential notes), it is usual to double the bass, which is the *fifth* of the triad.

The **cadential** $^6_4$, which always comes on a stronger beat than its $^5_3$ resolution, is set out like this:

The same progression written with appoggiaturas looks like this and shows the leaning notes on the stronger beat. Only the chords of I and IV are found as cadential $^6_4$s.

10 Another use of the $^6_4$ chord is that of a passing chord on a weak beat between two positions of I and IV. The bass or fifth of the chord is still doubled.

It results from the vertical coincidence of contrary motion passing notes (here in the bass and tenor) and of a neighbouring note (in the soprano). The alto remains stationary.

11 A second inversion is sometimes found as part of a bass arpeggio along with the root position and first inversion of the same chord. Following the appearance of the $^6_4$ chord, the bass moves to another position of the same chord or by step to a new chord.

12 $^6_4$ chords over tonic or dominant can result from the use of parallel neighbouring notes.

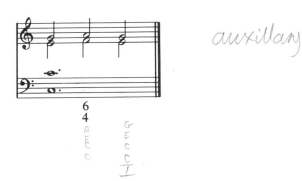

auxillary

135

Annotated examples for IV D

Haydn: 'The heavens are telling' from *The Creation*

1   Open score, i.e. one part per stave. Tenor sounds octave lower than written.
2   Dominant anacrusis in octaves.
3   Vibrant doubling of third of major chord (fifth omitted). High leap in tenor gives added brilliance.
4   First inversion dominant.
5   First inversion tonic. Contrary motion between soprano and bass.
6   II chord in root position as approach to V forming imperfect cadence.
7   3 bars orchestral interlude (voices rest).

8 Scalewise movement in contrary motion with bass, contrasting with more chordal movement of first phrase. Alto gives stability with repeated Gs.

9 V_2^4 dropping to I_6 (see Section E).

10 Double suspension (see Section J). Soprano and tenor are left suspended (on the dot), over the bass C, ultimately resolving on the fourth beat with notes of tonic chord. The alto G is common to both chords.

11 Standard II_6, $I\,{}^6_4$, V, I cadential progression.

Easter Hymn (adapted from *Lyra Davidica*, 1708)

1   Smoother bass line by use of V_6 rather than root position V.
2   Unusual overlapping of parts.
3   First inversion of subdominant.
4   Plagal cadence IV – I across bar line, with tonic chord decorated with IV $\frac{6}{4}$ on first beat.
5   Passing notes in bass and soprano over held chord.
6   Second inversion dominant 7th (see Section E) with a suspended C (see Section J).
7   Cadential $\frac{6}{4}$ decorating perfect cadence. In tenor, notice placing of F (the seventh of the dominant chord) on fourth beat.
8   Modulation (at start of phrase) into dominant key of G.
9   VII_6 between I and I_6 in G.
10 Modulation back to C with aid of third inversion dominant 7th.
11 VII_6 between I_6 and I (now in key of C).
12 'Alleluia chorus' in key of G.
13 Powerful use of last inversion of dominant 7th moving down to I_6 (see Section E).
14 Unusual doubling of note C (root of chord) in $\frac{6}{4}$ – $\frac{5}{3}$ progression.

E   The dominant seventh and its resolution

1   The root position of the dominant 7th usually resolves on to the root position of the tonic chord. In four-part harmony, the fifth of one chord or the other is omitted in this progression.

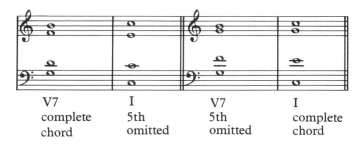

V7	I	V7	I
complete	5th	5th	complete
chord	omitted	omitted	chord

2   When at the end of a piece it is especially desirable to have a complete chord, the leading note, or third of the dominant, may move down to the fifth of the tonic chord if it occurs in an inside part. (Bach favoured this practice.)

Bach: *Christus, der ist mein Leben*

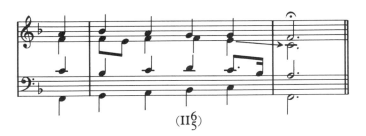

(II$^6_5$)

3   The dominant 7th has three inversions.

As with the root position, the tritone in the chord is restricted in its resolution, and normally the seventh moves downwards and the third (or leading note) moves up by a semitone.

root position	1st inversion	2nd inversion	3rd inversion

Because in each of the three inversions the root of V$_7$ appears in an upper part, it is able to remain stationary and become the fifth of the tonic chord. There is no need to omit the fifth of either chord.

4   The seventh of the chord does *not* fall in the following contexts:
   a When the resolution is not to the tonic and the seventh is taken into the next chord.

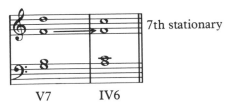

7th stationary

V7   IV6

139

b When the seventh moves to another note before resolving.

c When the second inversion appears between I and I₆ and an upper part moves in parallel motion with the bass.

d When the dominant chord is repeated and the seventh (unless it is in the bass) moves to another part.

F Cadences in four parts

1 There are four basic types of cadence.
   a Perfect cadence V(₇) – I

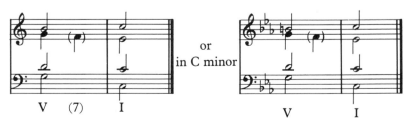

or
in C minor

Except at the end of a piece, one or other chord in a perfect cadence may appear as a first inversion. The sound of such a cadence is less final.

Pieces in the minor sometimes end with a major tonic triad.

The natural in the figuring under the final chord refers to the raised third, which is called a **tierce de Picardie** ('Picardy third'). This practice dates from the Renaissance, a period when it was considered unacceptable to end on a minor chord, so either the third of the chord was omitted altogether or it was raised to form a major chord.

The dominant chord is often decorated with a double appoggiatura resulting in a $^6_4$ chord.

b Plagal cadence IV – I

As with the perfect cadence, this may be used as the final cadence at the end of a piece.

Associated with 'Amen' in sacred music,

The tonic note is often found repeated in the upper voice.

Occasionally plagal cadences are found with II$_6$ substituted for IV.

A perfect cadence is sometimes extended by decorating the tonic chord with appoggiaturas, resulting in a IV $^6_4$ chord.

 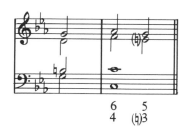

Although this has the effect of a plagal cadence, it is, strictly speaking, a decorated perfect cadence, and is often given a *tierce de Picardie*.

c Interrupted cadence V – VI

When the chord of VI is substituted for I at a cadence the resulting sound is a surprise, and the forward drive of the phrase towards a conclusion is arrested.

Third doubled
avoiding
consecutive 5ths
between bass
and soprano

Aptly named an **interrupted cadence**, it is known in the USA as a 'deceptive cadence'.

In the minor key, the chord of VI is a major triad and is less striking. It is usual to double the major third in the V – VI progression in the minor key. It is often found at the end of the penultimate phrase, where it holds up the progression of the music towards a final cadence.

Following V at a cadence point, any replacement of the chord of I by another chord can be classed as an interrupted cadence. Chromatic chords (i.e. chords which include notes not in the key itself) are much used in this context.

d Imperfect cadence

Any cadence which has the dominant as its second chord may be classed as an **imperfect cadence**. The effect is always inconclusive. The most common imperfect cadences are II$_6$ – V and IV – V.

In IV – V it is best to allow the three upper parts to move in contrary motion to the bass.

In minor imperfect cadences, avoid the interval of an augmented 2nd by not using the sixth and raised seventh degrees of the scale in the same part.

143

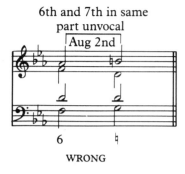

6th and 7th in same
part unvocal

Aug 2nd

6

♮

WRONG

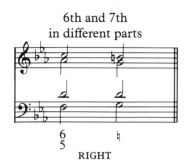

6th and 7th
in different parts

6
5

♮

RIGHT

2 Perfect and plagal cadences should not be approached through the tonic chord, especially in root position, as it detracts from the effect of the cadence.

Find examples of hymns and chorales and note the types of cadence used at the end of each line. Remember that modulation may occur, indicated in four-part harmony by the use of accidentals. Look out for the leading note in the new key as a guide.

Write out cadences of all types in four parts in a variety of keys. Sketch in the bass and soprano and then fill in the inside parts. Try to *imagine* the sound of what you write, before playing it. In cadences other than imperfect ones, place the second chord on a strong beat.

Wherever possible, use an approach chord which is different from the cadence chords.

G Chord choice

1 When constructing a chord framework, think in phrases which progress towards suitable cadences, e.g.

  1st phrase – imperfect cadence
  2nd phrase –perfect cadence (perhaps in dominant)
  3rd phrase – interrupted cadence
  4th phrase – perfect cadence (perhaps with *tierce de Picardie* if in the
          minor), or alternatively a plagal cadence.

2 Approach the cadence with appropriate chords. If possible avoid either of the cadence chords, especially in root position. The final chord of the cadence will normally come on a strong beat except when delayed with a ⁶₄ chord, e.g.

  Choose I, II or VI to approach a IV – V imperfect cadence
  Choose I or IV to approach an interrupted cadence
  Choose II, IV or sometimes VI to approach a perfect cadence and
  Avoid IV and I when approaching a plagal cadence.

3   Except at the beginning, do not repeat a chord across a bar line (weak – strong).

4   Consider an increase in the rate of chord change just before the cadence. This is particularly desirable in instrumental music, where the rate of chord change is often just once a bar, which may be increased to two or three changes per bar when approaching a cadence.

5   Use first inversions to give a more melodic bass line, to soften the effect of the chord and to avoid the parallel voice-leading which often arises when a progression is confined to root positions.

6   For strong progressions, choose chords with roots a fourth or fifth apart, such as V – I.

| V | I | I | IV | II | V | III | VI | VI | II |

IV – VII (VII – IV) embraces the tritone and is best avoided.

7   For smooth progressions, choose chords with roots a third apart (as with the substitute chords).
    When they move in a downward direction they may be used without restriction, but in an upwards direction they should only be used where the second chord falls on a weaker beat of the bar.

| I | VI | VI | IV | V | III | IV | II |

The smoothness of such downward progressions arises from the fact that the new chord takes over two of the previous notes of the triad, and at the same time provides a new bass note. The value of such a progression also arises from the fact that it is leading (via chord II and by implication V) towards the tonic chord.

| I | VI | IV | II |

145

Similarly, in the upward progression, two notes are shared between chords a third apart. But this time the bass note of the second chord is not new, but is the third (the weakest note of the triad) of the first chord.

8 Chords whose roots lie a second apart have no sounds in common, and should therefore be used only when their particular effect is required. Remember that an interrupted cadence falls into this category and upward steps sound more convincing than downward. In either case voice-leading often leads to parallels, so take care.

9 Second inversions I $\frac{6}{4}$ and IV $\frac{6}{4}$ should be used at cadence points on a *stronger* beat than the following chord, which should have the same bass note. Occasionally they may be used as passing, arpeggio or neighbouring-note chords. All these occur on a weaker beat and arise from voice-leading.

10 The dominant 7th should be used sparingly (mostly for perfect and interrupted cadences) and should not be substituted for the chord of V at every opportunity. Remember also the value of VII_6 as a substitute chord.

H Matching melodies

As you gain experience in harmonization you will use a wide variety of chords to express your ideas. However, in the early stages you should aim at becoming fluent in the use of a few well-tried progressions associated with commonly-recurring melodic fragments, such as the following. Of these alternative harmonizations (indicated by the additional bass parts), the first of each may be regarded as the most versatile.

a Down to the tonic

or with an octave jump

b Up from the tonic

I   V   I

I   V 6   I

or with an inversion

c To or from the mediant

I6   VII6   I

I6   V$\frac{4}{3}$ I

I6   V$\frac{6}{4}$ I

or with
2nd inversion
dominant 7th

or with
passing $\frac{6}{4}$

I   VII6   I6

I   V$\frac{4}{3}$ I6

I   V$\frac{6}{4}$ I6

d Rising to the tonic

IV   VII6   I(6)

II6   V   I(6)

IV or II6   V$\frac{4}{2}$ I6

V$\frac{4}{2}$ must fall to I6
not to root position.

or with
Supertonic

or with last
inversion dominant 7th

IV H

e Stressing the tonic

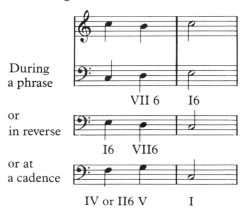

During a phrase

VII 6   I6

or in reverse

I6   VII6

or at a cadence

IV or II6 V   I

f Dropping from the tonic

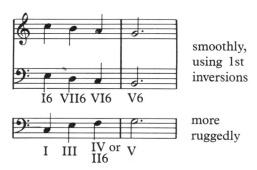

smoothly, using 1st inversions

I6 VII6 VI6   V6

more ruggedly

I   III   IV or II6   V

g To or from the subdominant

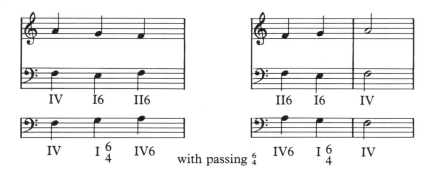

IV   I6   II6

IV   I $^6_4$ IV6

with passing $^6_4$

II6   I6   IV

IV6   I $^6_4$ IV

h To or from the dominant

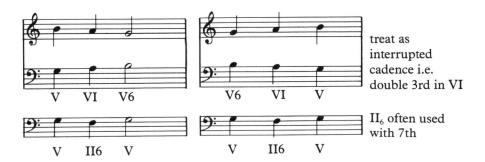

V   VI   V6

V6   VI   V

treat as
interrupted
cadence i.e.
double 3rd in VI

V   II6   V

V   II6   V

II$_6$ often used
with 7th

I Non-chord notes in four-part harmony

1 Passing notes (both unaccented and accented) as well as appoggiaturas and neighbouring notes may be used in four-part harmony. The same conditions of movement by step between chord notes apply as were stated in II E. However, where there are more than two parts, additional care is needed in order to avoid unintentional clashes and harmonic confusion.
Use unessential or non-chord notes discreetly in early exercises. Their use in more complex contexts, such as the chorale harmonizations of Bach, may be intensely expressive.

2 Remember that passing notes and other non-chord notes must connect two harmony notes. They must not move other than by step.

3 In four-part harmony, the following points should be observed:
  a Passing notes may occur in more than one part at a time provided that they move in parallel thirds and sixths or pass through the same note by contrary motion.

passes through the same note

Parallel thirds   Parallel sixths   Same note taken in
                                            contrary motion

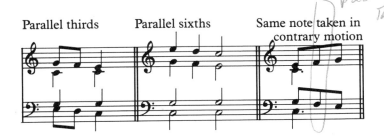

b Passing notes should not produce a semitone clash (even in different octaves) with a harmony note already sounding.

Such clashes can usually be avoided by the use of a further passing note, e.g.

c Take care that by adding a passing note you do not spoil an otherwise correct passage of voice-leading.

If quaver movement is really necessary in such a passage, a chordal skip is often a more satisfactory solution.

d Avoid running a passing note into a chord note.

4   Accented passing notes (which must also move stepwise) and appoggiaturas, or leaning notes, are most effective when descending. They must fall on a stronger beat than the note they replace and must sound with the remaining notes of the chord.

5   Accented passing notes may only be sounded *against* their note of resolution in the following contexts:
     a If the note of resolution comes in the bass.

or **b** if the note of resolution is approached by step in contrary motion.

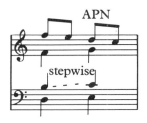

6 Accented passing notes may be doubled in parallel thirds and sixths, especially when they fill the gap between chord notes. In this form they sound well ascending.

7 Neighbouring notes may be used both between appearances of the same chord and between different chords. They may be doubled in thirds and sixths.

8 Where a beat subdivides, it is nearly always better, except in the case of a chordal skip, to treat the note which subdivides the beat as an unessential note rather than as a harmony note.

9 In a minor key, in order to avoid an augmented 2nd, passing notes which embrace the sixth and seventh degrees should use one or the other form of the melodic minor scale.

  a Over the dominant chord, use the raised sixth in conjunction with the leading note, both descending and ascending.

152

b And over IV or VI use the flattened seventh in conjunction with the sixth whether up or down.

Annotated examples for IV I

J. Hatton: *Duke Street*

1 Chord VI followed on same bass note by chord IV_6.
The crotchet chord changes in this hymn are all linked with two syllables in the text.
2 Slurred crotchets are treated as based on the same chord and carry one syllable.
3 Passing notes C sharp (soprano) and E (tenor) over chord of IV.
4 C sharp now appears as accented passing note, also over chord IV.
5 Second inversion dominant 7th ($V\,^4_3$) between I and I_6, the seventh of the chord in the tenor part rising in parallel thirds with the bass.
6 VII_6 between I_6 and I.
7 Chordal skips.

8 Passing notes in thirds.
9 VII₆ used between IV and I.
10 Bass **melisma** (several notes sung to the same syllable).
11 Typical dropping octave in bass to I $^6_4$ V cadence progression.

Bach: *Auf meinen lieben Gott*

1 Smooth bass line with V₆ in G minor.
2 Chordal skip in tenor.
3 Imperfect cadence IV₆ – V in G minor.
4 Bass moves down one degree to change V into V$^4_2$.
5 Then proceeds to I₆.
6 Short suspension of G resolving into F sharp in chord of VII₆.
   (Could also be described as a neighbouring note figure over II₇.)
7 Another imperfect cadence, this time II₆ – V. (II in G minor is a diminished chord.)

8   Move toward B flat confirmed at cadence in next bar.

9   Passing notes in bass.

10   Alto B flat has been prepared in the same part of the previous chord and can be regarded either as a suspended note resolving a step downwards on the next beat to A, or as the seventh of the chord of the supertonic 7th resolving II_6 – V in the key of B flat. Whichever explanation is adopted, it should be noted that this progression is characteristic of Bach's style.

11   Intentionally high tenor.

12   Neighbouring notes in parallel sixths in alto and tenor occurring on the beat over chord V in F major.

13   Accented passing note in bass – a favourite expressive device of Bach.

14   As with 10 above, the alto G may be regarded as either a suspension, or as the 7th of the supertonic 7th in G minor.

15   Alto F sharp (leading note) moves down to the fifth of the final chord instead of to the tonic (for fullness of effect).

16   B natural changes tonic chord to major, an example of a *tierce de Picardie*.

J   Suspensions

1   A **suspension** is a close relative of both the accented passing note and the appoggiatura, or leaning note. Each provides a discord on a strong or stronger part of the beat, but each is approached differently.

   a   An accented passing note moves by step.

   b   A leaning note or appoggiatura falls on a stronger beat, or part of the beat, than its resolution and moves either downward by step or, more rarely, up by a semitone. It may be approached from any other note.

   c   A suspension may be likened to an appoggiatura which has been approached, or *prepared*, from the *same* note on the preceding beat.

2   In a suspension, a note is held across (or repeated) in the same voice part from a chord on a weak beat, to form a **discord** (point of tension) on the strong beat. This is then followed by its resolution on the succeeding weak beat or part of the beat. The suspended note is sometimes, but not necessarily, tied to the preparatory note. It must not sound against its note of resolution unless that note comes in the bass.

This:

but not this:

3   When a suspension is figured it shows the interval above the bass of the discord and of its resolution.

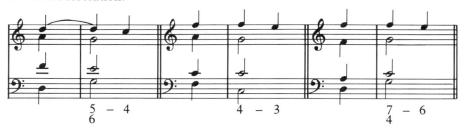

4   A suspension sometimes resolves upwards by a semitone from leading note to tonic, in which case it may be termed a **retardation**.

5   A suspension may be effectively used in the bass, but is best limited to resolutions on to the *third* of the chord. This note should not be doubled in an upper part.

6 As with other non-chord notes, suspensions can move to adjacent notes, or to other chord notes before finally resolving.

Sometimes, particularly in instrumental music, the resolution may be delayed by several notes.

7 A suspension can appear in an inside part.

8 Suspensions may occur in two or three parts at the same time.

9 The position of a suspension is usually indicated by the occurrence of a weak to strong held or repeated note, followed by a note one step lower which forms a consonance with the bass or lowest note.

K Modulation

1 As we saw in II 1, most pieces longer than a few bars contain a modulation to a closely related key.

2 A modulation in a melody may be implied without the use of a note foreign to the tonic key. In four-part harmony it may be assumed that a modulation has not been defined *unless* a note foreign to the tonic has been introduced.

3 A modulation is usually established by a perfect or an interrupted cadence in the new key. This will often happen at the end of a phrase.

IV K 1 to 5

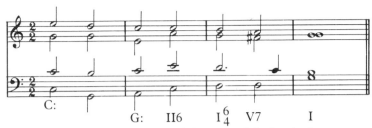

C:

G: II6   I$^6_4$ V7   I

The crucial chord which establishes a modulation is, however, not the tonic of the new key, but chord V (or V⁷ or VIIb) in the new key, in any inversion.

4 A cadence is often best approached through chord II in the *new* key. (Alternatively, IV or VI in the new key may be used.) This chord may or may not be common to both keys. If it is, it is termed a **pivot chord** (see II, I5).

a Modulation to dominant

C major to G major

C:

VI6

G: II6   V7   I

b Modulation to relative major

A minor to C major

Am: IV6

C: II6   V7   I

c Modulation to relative minor

C major to A minor

C:

IV

Am: VI   II   V   I

5   If possible, avoid using the note which is to be altered in any immediately
     preceding chord, e.g.
         In (a) above the note F is avoided after the up-beat in readiness for the change
                 to F sharp in the new key.
         In (b) G sharp appears only in the up-beat.
         In (c) G appears only in the first bar.

Annotated example for IV K

W. Croft: *Hanover*

1 Strong arpeggio bass line embracing I_6.
2 Contrasting minor substitute chords VI and II_6.
3 Move towards dominant. II_7 in D followed on last crotchet by VII_6.
   Tonic chord in next bar results in perfect cadence in D, but in a weaker form than at
4 Full/perfect cadence V – I in D.
5 Straight on to V – I in E minor (relative minor of G) for next phrase.
6 E minor chord is supertonic of D, so acts as pivot chord for modulation back to dominant.
7 Tenor D is suspended on the dot over change of chord to VII_6.
   Resolves on to C sharp to complete chord.
8 Straight back to G major. Alto D prepared in previous chord and sounded on first beat as a suspension over chord of IV. Resolves as chord changes.
9 Strongly leaping melody contrasts with mostly stepwise movement of rest of hymn.

V Texture, timbre and transposition

A Texture

1   Hymn tunes have a continuous musical texture in four parts. Each part moves along in step with the others and the melody is usually on top. Music of this kind is termed **homophonic** from the Greek meaning 'same sound'. Any music in which the melody has a simple, chordal accompaniment is known as **homophonic**.

2   Where individual voices or instruments have greater independence, the texture is usually more open. The parts do not move along in step, but weave a web of sound which arises from the interplay of different rhythms and lines. Often the entries of individual voices or instruments are staggered. Such music is termed **polyphonic**, meaning 'many sounds'.

3   Polyphony and homophony are two broad textural divisions. Within these other textures arise when:
    a Parts are widely spaced .

Tchaikovsky: *Danse chinoise* (from *The Nutcracker*)

b Parts are clustered together

Brahms: *Symphony No. 4* (4th movement)

c When continuous lines are contrasted with intermittent lines

Borodin: *Polovtsian Dances* (No. 3)

d Legato with staccato

Mendelssohn: *Midsummer Night's Dream* (Overture)

Violins

Violas
Cells

Fl.
Ob.
Clar.

Hn.
Bsn.

e Sound is interspersed with silence or near silence

Shostakovich: *String Quartet No. 8* (4th movement)

Vln 1
Vln 2

Vla
Cello

Largo

ff

pp

f And when the number of voice parts or lines is increased or reduced.

Dvořák: *Sonatina for violin and piano, Op. 100* (4th movement)

All textures are further enhanced by their instrumental or vocal colour and dynamic level. It is perhaps worth noting in this context that a great deal of 20th-century music has been concerned more with texture and timbre than with the more traditional elements of melody, rhythm and harmony.

4   In hymn tunes and similar four-part vocal music, the density is mostly constant. In keyboard, chamber and orchestral music, as well as in more elaborate choral music, the number of voice parts is modified to give textural variety. Unison or octave passages are contrasted with thick chords in six or more parts:

Vaughan Williams: *Symphony No. 6* (4th movement)

or single lines may grow into fuller textures as extra voices or instruments enter.

Bach: *Magnificat (Gloria)*

5   Music may have any number of voice parts, ranging from a single line, as in an unaccompanied folk-song, to a 40-part motet by Tallis or the dense, subtly shift-ing, many-voiced instrumental textures of the Hungarian composer Ligeti.

However, music in four parts may be considered as the norm (probably because of its association with vocal writing), while five parts are quite common, and much keyboard (and other instrumental) music has just a three-part texture.

Study examples of music which expands and contracts between one, two, three, four and more parts and listen to the sound of these and other textural contrasts.

B Three-part writing

1   As with two-part writing, the bass line is all-important, but now it must interact and make good harmonic sense with *two* upper parts.

2   The upper parts may be:
    a Closely linked and in rhythmic unison (often found in keyboard music).

Mendelssohn: *Andante and Rondo Capriccioso*

b Or more independent as in this example, where the viola completes the harmony, yet moves with more freedom than is often possible in four-part harmony.

Mozart: *Divertimento, K563*

c Or be melodically related but independent in movement; such textures are called **contrapuntal**.

Morley: *Cease mine Eyes* (bar 14)

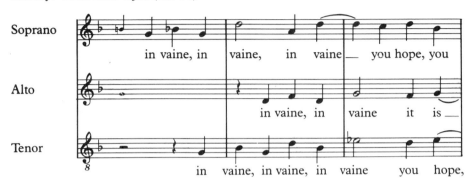

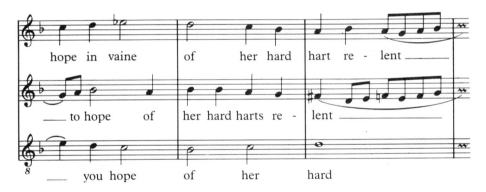

In all these cases, some conversation and exchange of ideas between the parts is usual.

3 As in two-part writing, extensive use of first inversions and chordal skips makes for an interesting bass and helps to clarify certain harmonic progressions.

4 Non-chord notes will allow the development of flowing parts and should be treated as in four-part harmony.

5 As in four-part harmony, unless for reasons of texture or voice-leading, the wider spacing should occur between the lower parts.

6 Parallel motion in octaves and fifths should be avoided unless for textural contrast. When such textures occur (as in the Mozart example above), they are care-

167

fully controlled. The continuous doubling of a part in octaves for reasons of strength or texture is quite different from the chance occurrence of a pair of unintentional octaves.

7 Exposed intervals between bass and either part should be avoided by approaching any single perfect fifth or octave by step in the upper part involved.

NB The following sections aim to give a brief introduction to instrumental writing. Further information and help should be obtained from reference books, from performers and from concentrated listening to particular instruments.

C Writing for the piano

1 The piano has a wide range

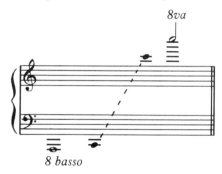

which is brilliant at the top and generally rather heavy in the extreme bass. The middle four octaves or so are the most versatile. Below the bass stave close intervals such as seconds and thirds are best avoided, or at least reserved for special effects.

2 Long notes (especially high ones) fade quickly. They are most effective when supported or reinforced with chords and figurations containing sympathetic notes. These help to keep them ringing.

3   Occasional chordal passages sound well. They should not be too thick in the lower register. Flowing figurations are the stock-in-trade of piano writing. They should lie well under the hands. Care should be taken to see that no passage involves an impossibly wide stretch.

4   The **sustaining pedal** (i.e. the right foot pedal) lifts all the dampers and allows the sound to continue until it is released. It is particularly useful for holding on to bass notes when the left hand jumps upwards to play other notes.

5   Any texture from single notes to chordal passages can be effective on the piano. Most notes may be freely doubled, but avoid doubling the major third of a chord and other notes of restricted movement such as the leading note and seventh of a chord, if they already occur in the bass.

6   When writing a piano piece, it is best at first to plan a chordal framework with perhaps one or two chords to the bar. Sketch in the upper two or three parts (as in vocal writing) and check that the voice-leading does not result in accidental parallel fifths and octaves (especially with adjacent root position chords). Once the framework is established, consider ways of laying out the harmonies between the hands. In general, once a figuration has been established, it will continue for most of the phrase, and any variation will occur at, or just before, the cadence.

7   Here are some typical piano figurations built on the progression I – VI – II$_6$ – II in three and more parts.

a   Vocal harmony in three parts.

b   Split between hands on the piano.

c

As broken chords.

d

Filled out with an extra part which still has correct voice-leading.

e

More agitated, with bass enlivened by rests and a slight change of figure at beginning of bar 2.

f

More elaborate version, with neighbouring notes.

g

Reiterated chords with octave doubling in left hand. Notice passing note G at end of bar 1, propelling passage forward.

passing note pushing passage on

Triple time (waltz) figuration.

Bass notes repeated with alternating chords. Notice octave displacement in bar 2. II₆ and II occur in bar 3.

Long note sustained and reinforced by arpeggio figure.

Arpeggio triplets. Third of chord missing at beginning of bar 2.

8 Although examples (e), (g), (h) and (i) include rests in the left hand, the effect of the bass prevails until the next note appears in the *same register.*

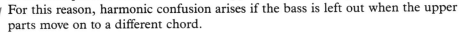 For this reason, harmonic confusion arises if the bass is left out when the upper parts move on to a different chord.

Here the effect produced is of two chords sounding at the same time with the chord of G being superimposed, first on that of C major and then on A minor.

By completing the bass line, such confusion is avoided.

Note that, although this problem often occurs in piano music, the same considerations apply to music for other instruments.

9   However, the tension which arises from the mixing of two chords may sometimes be deliberately exploited by maintaining the first bass note as a drone or **pedal point**. (This has nothing to do with the pedals on the piano, but refers to the foot, Latin *ped*, of a passage.)

(Notice the slight variation of figuration before the cadence.)

   Such pedal points are not confined to keyboard music and are sometimes extended over many bars. The transition from the third to the fourth movement of Beethoven's Symphony No. 5 is a famous example of a dominant pedal point. The only restriction is that the bass note must be part of both the first and last chords of the passage.

Beethoven: *Piano Sonata Op. 13* (bar 157)

D Pianoforte accompaniment

1   The piano is frequently used as an accompanying instrument for both voices and instruments.

2   In this role it sometimes outlines or reflects the solo line at the unison or octave (especially in songs).

Beethoven: *An die Geliebte*

3   The bass line must make good sense with the solo part and not produce consecutive octaves or fifths.

4 The piano accompaniment should be complete in itself. To this end, major 3rds (including the leading note as part of the dominant chord) and restricted intervals like 7ths may appear simultaneously in the accompaniment as well as in the solo part.

Schubert: *An die Musik*

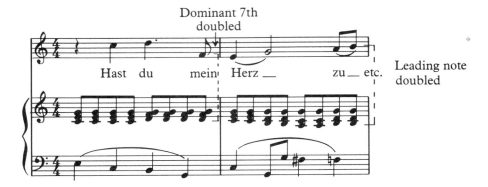

5 As with piano writing in general, the figuration should be consistent in style and should not produce undesirable parallels.

E Guitar Accompaniment

1 To write a fully notated accompaniment for the guitar requires a good working knowledge of the instrument.

2 However, by indicating the chord structure and style of playing, the student can provide a framework for a straightforward accompaniment which the guitarist can elaborate if desired.

The following suggestions offer ways of showing the chords and their figuration.

Write out the melody to be accompanied and with the help of Chapters II and III select suitable chords. Avoid keys with more than a single flat. Write the root name of each chord (e.g. G, D₇, E min(or)) above the stave, at the beginning of each bar or part of a bar where a chord-change occurs. Do not change chords unnecessarily.

3   Many guitarists do not use inversions, preferring the fullest or most convenient form of the chord even when this may result in an undesirable progression, as in the indiscriminate use of second inversions.

However, the discreet use of inversions can greatly enhance the accompaniment and the vitality of the bass line. They may be shown either with the use of standard figuring (e.g. G_6, D_4^6), or by adding the actual bass note to be played as a lower case (small letter) under the chord name (e.g. $\overset{G}{b}$ or $\overset{D}{a}$).

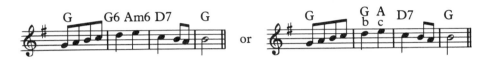

4   Show at the beginning the right-hand finger style,

  a in words, e.g. 'strum', 'pluck', etc.,

  b in diagrammatic form on a six-line stave representing the six strings of the guitar,

  c or as a single bar of notation indicating the figuration of the first chord.

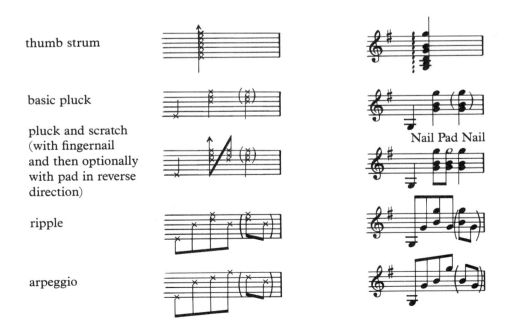

thumb strum

basic pluck

pluck and scratch (with fingernail and then optionally with pad in reverse direction)

Nail Pad Nail

ripple

arpeggio

Notice that in each case the sixth string (or, with some chords, the fifth or fourth string) is played at the beginning of the bar, followed by the upper three strings.

5   Guitar chords are often shown in diagrammatic form.

Dots represent the position of the fingers on the frets and a cross indicates that a string is not to be played. The easier chords, some of which are shown below, make use of open strings – sometimes, as with G, at the expense of a well-spaced chord.

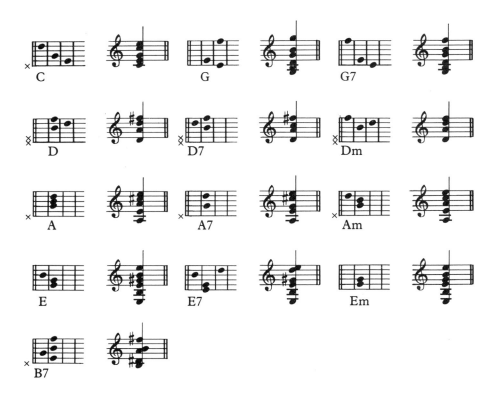

6   In notation, the guitar is treated as a tenor instrument and is written in the treble clef an octave higher than it sounds.

F Writing for strings

1 A reasonable working range for the instruments of the string family is as follows:

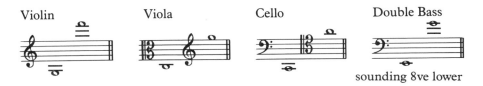

(All can play higher than the top notes marked, especially the violin and cello.)

Unless the strings are tuned to different pitches (known as *scordatura*), only the double bass is capable of playing notes lower than those indicated, by means of a fifth string or an extension mechanism.

2 Except for the double bass, the four strings are tuned a fifth apart. The highest is called the first string. Double bass strings are tuned a fourth apart. String players produce notes by stopping the strings with the left hand, which moves up the finger board to obtain higher notes. Each position of the left hand produces a different set of notes across the four strings. On the violin, first, third and fifth positions are as follows. (The first finger, as with all instruments other than keyboard instruments, is the index or pointing finger.)

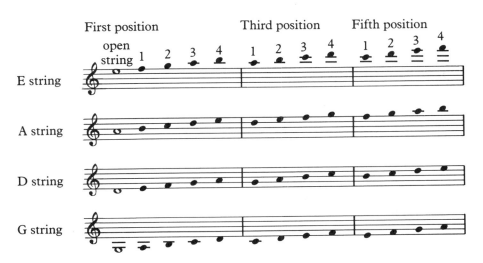

Sharps and flats are produced by slight forward and backward finger positions. Although accomplished players change position fluently, it is as well to avoid unnecessary shifts. Across the strings, one position can produce a range of over two octaves, but on any one string of only a fourth.

The viola is similar, but tuned a fifth lower. The cello and double bass have considerably longer strings, making it impossible for the hand to cover even the interval of a fourth. This results in more frequent changes of position.

3 String players play each note with one stroke of the bow, unless otherwise indicated. They normally draw the bow across the strings alternately down and up. Where necessary, these bowing movements are indicated by signs over the notes.

down   up

The up-bow tends to be a lighter stroke, and is used for up-beat starts to phrases unless these need special emphasis.

Frequent bow changes (one bow to a note) can be played smoothly, but more often produce a detached (*détaché*) effect.

4 When more than one note is to be played in a single bow-stroke, a slur is added.

Mozart: *Symphony No. 40 in G minor, K440*

5 When dots are added under a slur, the player slightly detaches the notes by a momentary stop in the bow-stroke.

Beethoven: *String Quartet, Op. 18, No. 5*

6 When dashes are added under slurs, the player slightly stresses the notes by finger pressure on the bow.

Dvořák: *Piano Quintet, Op. 81*

7   A note at the end of a slurred scale passage is played in the same bow.

Richard Strauss: *Don Quixote*

8   In bowing a passage, the notes taken in an up-bow should occupy the same time
as those taken in a down-bow, otherwise the player will either 'run out' of bow,
or will have to compensate with an increase of bow speed and therefore of tone.
For this reason, compound time and dotted rhythm passages are usually bowed
like this:

Haydn: *Symphony No. 94*

9   Strings are sometimes *plucked* with the fingers instead of being bowed. This is
called *pizzicato*, and is marked with the abbreviation *pizz*. When the bow is to
be resumed, the part is marked *arco*. Experienced players can change quickly
between one and the other.

10   Occasional chords (known in string-playing as *double* and *triple stops*) are effective. Without a thorough knowledge of the instrument, it is best to play safe and
limit the chords used to those containing one or two open (i.e. unstopped)
strings.

11   Mutes may be placed on the bridge of a string instrument to reduce and modify
the tone. When this quality of sound is required, the part is marked *con sordino*
(*con sord*.). When the mutes are to be removed, the part is marked *senza sordino*.
Sufficient time (i.e. several bars rest) should be allowed for both operations.

12   String players, especially beginners, play most happily in the keys of G, D and
A. Their instruments are most resonant in these keys because of the open
strings.

G Writing for woodwind

1 Each instrument of the woodwind family has a distinct tonal quality. The different registers of each instrument add further variety to these qualities. Familiarity with these tone-colours can only be gained from extensive listening experience, but the summaries listed below the ranges will help aural awareness. Less proficient woodwind players have difficulty with production and control at the extremities of the compass. The crotchet heads under brackets indicate a reasonably practical working range.

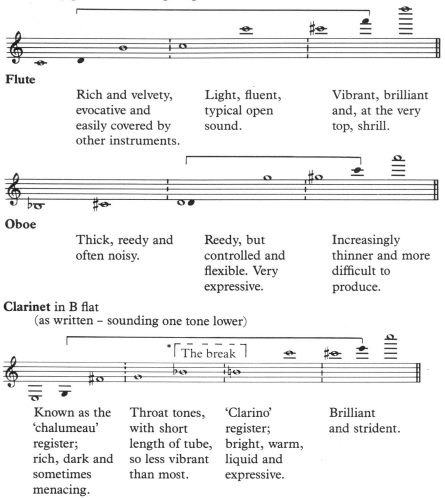

Flute

Rich and velvety, evocative and easily covered by other instruments.	Light, fluent, typical open sound.	Vibrant, brilliant and, at the very top, shrill.

Oboe

Thick, reedy and often noisy.	Reedy, but controlled and flexible. Very expressive.	Increasingly thinner and more difficult to produce.

Clarinet in B flat
(as written – sounding one tone lower)

Known as the 'chalumeau' register; rich, dark and sometimes menacing.	Throat tones, with short length of tube, so less vibrant than most.	'Clarino' register; bright, warm, liquid and expressive.	Brilliant and strident.

*NB Problems arise with passages written over 'the break' where the lower note is a short length of tube using few fingers and the upper note uses all the fingers and the full length of the tube.

Bassoon

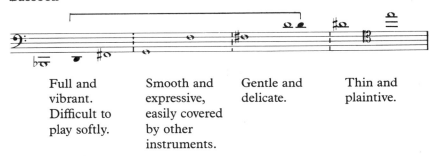

| Full and vibrant. Difficult to play softly. | Smooth and expressive, easily covered by other instruments. | Gentle and delicate. | Thin and plaintive. |

2   All four instruments have larger and smaller relatives, especially the clarinet which has several. They have similar ranges, play from the same written notes, but **transpose** to a higher or lower sound. (See section H.)

3   Wind instruments are equally at home with agile scale passages and expressive lines. The double-reed instruments (oboe and bassoon) are slightly less flexible but have a superior power of attack.

4   When writing for wind, remember that the players need to breathe. Do not, therefore, write continuous fast or sustained passages which have no rests or natural breaks in the phrases. Oboe players in particular need occasional longer rests to recover from the physical exertion of playing.

5   Wind players 'tongue' (or articulate) each note separately unless an added slur indicates otherwise. Woodwind articulation is very important and phrasing (i.e. the grouping of notes under slurs, or staccato notes) should be precisely indicated.

Bartók: *Concerto for Orchestra* (4th movement)

Upward slurs are mostly easy to play, but downward slurs can be tricky.

H Writing for brass

1   Like woodwind players, brass players need time to breathe. In longer pieces
    they too need longer periods for physical recovery, especially to rest their lips.
    Brass players constantly re-position their lips to produce notes, and long
    passages consequently become very tiring.

2   As with woodwind music, articulation is very important and such details as slurs
    and staccato marks must be added. Rapidly repeated notes are particularly effec-
    tive on the trumpet. They are sometimes played by means of **double** or **triple
    tonguing**.

3   *Unlike* woodwind instruments, the tone-quality of the different members of the
    brass family is similar although trumpets tend to be brilliant, horns are more
    mellow, trombones rich and tubas rounded in tone. All are capable of an exten-
    sive dynamic range from very soft to very loud and strident. The horn is the
    least powerful. An *fp* (*forte-piano*, or *sforzando*) attack is particularly arresting on
    the brass.

Sibelius: *Symphony No. 1* (2nd movement)

4   Brass players do not have reeds but rely on their lips, in conjunction with the
    mouthpiece, to set up vibrations. As the lips tighten, higher sounds are
    produced, drawn from the harmonic series related to the length of the
    instrumental tube.

Some of these notes are out of tune with our scales and should be avoided where
possible (e.g. the seventh harmonic, which is flat).

5   All the above notes can be produced from the instrument's basic tube length
    without the use of valves or slides. (In practice, the fundamental tone is quite
    difficult to obtain, especially on the trumpet.

6　To sound other notes, the player lengthens the tube. Before the invention of valves, this was done by inserting a different-sized coil of tubing, called a **crook**, into the pipework. Each crook fixed the instrument in a different key, hence horn in E flat, trumpet in G, and so on. But to simplify matters, the player always played from a part in the key of C, leaving the size of the crook to determine which series of sounds emerged. Thus, with a crook in E flat, this series of notes would be possible:

 and so on.

This is the reason why to this day most brass instruments are **transposing** instruments. The exception is the trombone, which has always had an extendable crook (or **slide**) which permits the player to play perfectly in tune in any key. Each position of the slide gives a different series of harmonics.

 and so on.

I   II   III

Trumpet, horn, tuba and other brass instruments release a valve which introduces an additional length of tubing. There are three basic valves:

　the first of which lowers the instrument a tone (1 0 0)

　the second, or middle valve, a semitone (0 2 0)

　and the third valve lowers the instrument a tone and a half (0 0 3).

Combinations of valves allow the basic series to be lowered by up to an augmented 4th.

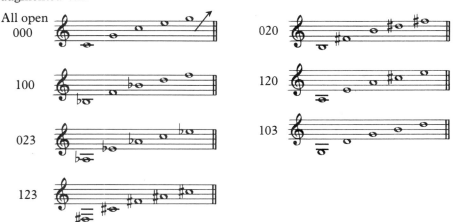

From this it will be seen that the greatest choice of fingering occurs in the upper register. Modern brass instruments sometimes have additional valves, or *pistons*, which either switch the instrument from, say, F to B flat (i.e. the double horn) or, especially on the tuba, allow slight adjustments to be made to the intonation.

7   The extent of the lower range of a brass instrument is subject to the ability of the player or his instrument to produce pedal notes. The upper limits are determined by the degree of lip tension a player can command. For most purposes, the following ranges will be found practical.

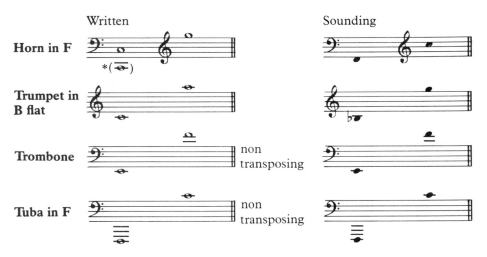

*   Confusingly, horn notes in the bass clef are sometimes written an octave lower, so that in the case of a horn in F they sound a perfect 4th higher, rather than a perfect 5th lower (as in the treble clef).

I   Transposing instruments and transposition

1   Quite a number of orchestral instruments, and many in brass or military bands, are *transposing instruments*.

2   Before the invention of valves on brass instruments and before the development of elaborate key systems for woodwind, many instruments were strictly limited in their choice of keys. This was either overcome by the use of crooks, as with the horn, or by having a number of instruments available, each of different size and pitch. So the clarinet at one time was found pitched in C, D, E flat, B flat and A: only the last two of these are normally found in orchestras now, although some of the others survive in military bands.

3 The practice of transposition arose so that the player should encounter no reading or fingering problems when he changed crooks or instruments.

4 Up until the second half of the 18th century, even timpani were treated as transposing instruments. They were always written in the key of C regardless of the actual tuning of the drums, which would have been the dominant and tonic of the key of the movement.

Bach: *Mass in B minor*

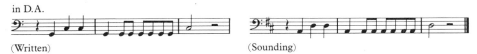

in D.A.

(Written)   (Sounding)

5 With the exception of instruments which transpose up or down an octave, such as the piccolo or double bass, and of the cor anglais which sounds a fifth lower than written, all instruments indicate by their name their transposing interval (e.g. horn in F).

    Remember this invariable rule:

        When the note C is *written*, the name of the instrument *sounds*, e.g. when C is notated and fingered on a clarinet in B flat, the sound B flat is produced. And when C is notated and fingered on a horn in E flat, the sound E flat is produced.

    The sound produced is sometimes referred to as **concert pitch** to distinguish it from **written pitch** (e.g. 'concert B flat').

6 Consequently, when G is *written* for a B flat instrument, the note a tone (or major 2nd) lower will sound, i.e. F, and when G is *written* for a horn in E flat, the note a major 6th lower will sound, i.e. B flat.

7 As will be seen from the following table, most instruments transpose downwards, but a few, for example trumpets in D, transpose upwards. The instruments in the first column are the most commonly found in an orchestra, and a selection of other transpositions is listed in the other columns. Instruments in C do not transpose other than to an octave above or below.

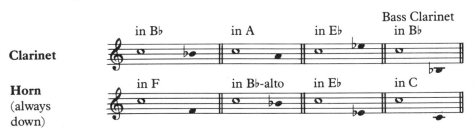

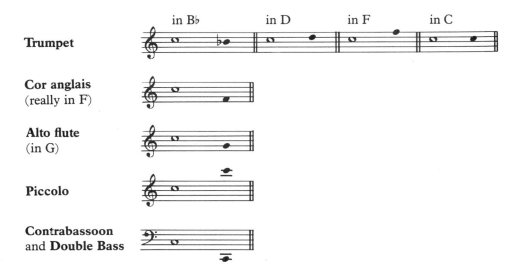

8 Parts for saxophones and members of the **cornet** family in brass bands are written for simplicity in the treble clef, regardless of their actual pitch. They are without exception B flat or E flat instruments, and some transpose down over two octaves. This allows players to switch from instrument to instrument without the complication of learning a new fingering or clef.

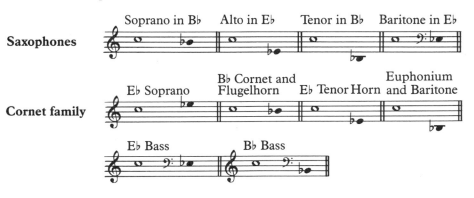

9 To write a part for a transposing instrument, work as follows:
   a Select the instrument and note its name, e.g. trumpet in B flat.
   b On a B flat trumpet, a written C sounds one tone lower, i.e. B flat.
   c Therefore write each note one tone or a major 2nd *higher* than the required sound.

 Tpt. in B♭

Sound required   Written one tone higher

10 In orchestral scores, horns and trumpets are usually written without key signatures, so accidentals have to be *added* to the part to make sure that each note is precisely at the correct pitch. Be careful about this – it is very easy to slip up, e.g. Sound required

written a 5th higher for horn in F without using accidentals,

would sound as

and would need to be corrected with a B flat in the horn part.

11 The convention of open key signatures is not observed with woodwind instruments.

When writing for clarinets or cor anglais, or when transposing a part for some other reason, such as the accommodation of a singer's vocal range, work as follows:

a Choose the instrument and decide on its transposing interval, for example, on the cor anglais a written C sounds a 5th lower as F.

b Therefore write each note a perfect fifth *higher* than the sound required.

c But, since a key signature is customary for cor anglais parts, first decide which key is a perfect 5th higher than the concert pitch or sound and then add its key signature.

Concert pitch required in key D

Written a 5th higher in key A

Cor Anglais

Key signature of D

Key signature of A

d Now only accidentals in the original or concert pitch will need special attention, e.g.

Written a 5th higher in E minor, with accidentals adjusted

Concert pitch in A minor

Cor Anglais

Open key
signature
(C or A minor)

One sharp
signature
(G or E minor)

Notice
flat in
original
becomes
natural

J   Orchestral scores

1   In the Renaissance period, instrumental ensembles were very varied, and often depended simply on the availability of instruments. There was no standard ensemble.

2   By the end of the 17th century, the bowed string group had become accepted as the basic ensemble, to which wind instruments were added either for reinforcement, or to play contrasting solo passages. Bach wrote many important parts for high trumpets and mostly placed their music along with the timpani at the top of the page. Flutes and oboes followed, then the strings, and finally the continuo parts which sometimes included bassoon.

3   By the late 18th century, trumpet and drum parts had been down-graded and became simpler, lower in pitch and written below the woodwind parts in the middle of the score. Strings remained at the bottom of the page and the continuo part gradually faded from the group. Percussion, in the form of Turkish music (drums, cymbals, triangle) was occasionally added to some scores for special effect.

4   In the 19th century, additional woodwind and brass instruments were used, including trombones and tuba, as part of the standard orchestra. Harps (absent since the early opera orchestras of the 17th century) returned with renewed vitality and the string group was considerably enlarged to provide a rich balanced sound. Percussion instruments became more numerous and diverse (though not all composers used them).

5   Once the orchestra had become more standardized at the end of the 18th century, the orchestral score was laid out in instrumental families which made it easier to follow. Within each family group the instruments were set out in descending order of pitch, with the exception of the piccolo. As this instrument was usually played by the second or third flute-player, it was placed (at first) below the first flute. The horns also, though lower in range than the trumpets, were placed next to the woodwind rather than below the trumpets.

6   The growth and development of the orchestra from the 18th to the 20th century can be traced through the five orchestras listed below:

Bach: *Magnificat* (1723)	Haydn: *Symphony No. 94* (1791)	Beethoven: *Symphony No. 9* (1823)	Berlioz: *Benvenuto Cellini* overture (1837)	Holst: *The Planets* suite (1915)
2 flutes	2 flutes	2 flutes piccolo	2 flutes (incl. piccolo)	4 flutes (incl. piccolo and bass flute)
2 oboes	2 oboes	2 oboes	2 oboes	3 oboes (incl. cor anglais)
		2 clarinets	2 clarinets	3 clarinets bass clarinet
	2 bassoons	2 bassoons contrabassoon	4 bassoons	3 bassoons double bassoon
	2 horns (in G)	4 horns (in D)	4 horns (in G, E and D)	6 horns
2 trumpets (in D)	2 trumpets (in C)	2 trumpets (in D)	4 trumpets (in G, E and D) 2 cornets in A	4 trumpets
		3 trombones	3 trombones ophicleide	3 trombones 2 tubas

timpani	timpani	timpani	timpani (2 players)	timpani (2 players)
		triangle	triangle	triangle
				side drum
				tambourine
		cymbals	cymbals	cymbals
		bass drum	bass drum	bass drum
				gong
				bells
				glockenspiel
				celeste
				2 harps
				organ
strings	strings	strings	strings	strings
continuo				
choir (SATB)		choir (SATB)		female choir (SA)

7 First and second wind instruments are written on one stave, except when this might lead to confusion. By and large, however, players of these instruments nowadays are provided with separate parts. When both instruments are to play in unison, the score is marked *a 2*, or alternatively the parts are given double stems. When the players have independent parts, the note-stems are turned up or down accordingly. A part is marked *1*, *I*, or *I°* when the first player is to play alone, and *2* or *II* similarly for the second player. If the part is very exposed, i.e. completely unsupported by the rest of the orchestra, the part is marked 'solo' as a warning.

8 Occasionally string parts are divided and the part is marked *divisi* or *div.* followed by *unis.* on the return to unison. *Div. a 4* implies that the part is to divide into 4 parts. A solo part for one string-player, or sub-group of players, is marked *tutti* at the point where all the players are to join in once more.

9 Some confusion arises over English, Italian, French and German names for instruments: the most commonly encountered are listed below.
 Note in particular that *corno* is *not* a cornet, and *tromba* is *not* a trombone.
 Be careful with the English abbreviations *vln* (violin), *vla* (viola), and *vlc* (for violoncello).

English	Italian	French	German
piccolo (picc.)	flauto piccolo	petite flûte	Kleine Flöte
flute (fl.)	flauto	grande flûte	Grosse Flöte
oboe (ob.)	oboe	hautbois	Hoboe
English horn (EH.)	corno inglese	cor anglais	Englisch Horn
clarinet (cl.)	clarinetto	clarinette	Klarinette
bassoon (bsn.)	fagotto	basson	Fagott
double bassoon (dbn.)	contra fagotto	contre basson	Kontrafagott
horn (hn.)	corno	cor	Horn
trumpet (tpt.)	tromba	trompette	Trompete
cornet (cnt., *not* cor.)	cornetto a pistoni	cornet-à-pistons	Cornett
trombone	trombone	trombone	Posaune
timpani (timp.)	timpani	timbales	Pauken
bass drum (b.dr.)	gran cassa	grosse caisse	Grosse Trommel
snare drum (s.dr.)	tamburo	tambour	Kleine Trommel
cymbals (cym.)	piatti	cymbales	Becken
tambourine (tamb.)	tamburino	tambour de Basque	Tamburin
triangle (tr.(gl.))	triangolo	triangle	Triangel
glockenspiel (gl.)	campanelli	carillon	Glockenspiel
xylophone (xyl.)	xylofono	xylophone	Xylophon
violin (vln.)	violino	violon	Violine
viola (vla.)	viola	alto	Bratsche
(violon)cello (vlc.)	violoncello	violoncelle	Violoncell
contra bass (cb.) (double bass) (db.) (bass)	contrabasso	contrebasse	Kontrabass

10 Following or extracting information from a score needs a quick eye, concentration and a knowledge of score layout. Below are a few hints to help improve score-reading ability.

a Start by looking at the score of a string quartet, or trio. Look through it at leisure before following it with the music.

b Move on to scores with more instruments.

c Learn to spot instrumental families (wind, brass, percussion and strings) which in most scores are bracketed together.

d Look out for clefs and key signatures which will help to identify instruments.

   i In the woodwind family, the clarinet will have a different key signature.

   ii In the brass, horns (often bracketed in two pairs) and trumpets will have no key signatures. Tenor trombones might have a tenor clef.

   iii Percussion instruments will usually be written on single lines rather than five-line staves.

   iv In the string group, violins 1 and 2 will be bracketed together, and the viola will have an alto clef.

e Note whether a complete score is printed on the page, or whether because there are fewer instruments playing, only part of the score is set out, followed by a further system of staves below it. In practice this can be confusing, as what at first may appear to be, say, five bars, is in fact five plus a further line of five bars below them. This practice also results in the string family appearing half-way up the page at the bottom of the first system. To assist the conductor or reader to spot such a layout, the division between the systems is sometimes marked with heavy lines at each end in addition to a slight space.

f Violin 1 is likely to have much of the melodic line. Follow this to start with, but keep your eyes moving upwards as well as forwards for interpolations and doubling on wind. Watch out for important woodwind lines, and look downwards for the all-important bass parts.

g In 18th- and early 19th-century scores, horns and trumpets will be confined largely to notes of the tonic chord set out in the key of C.

h When following a score, try to pick up the pulse so that your eye moves along with the music. If you get lost, move on to a page which has a noticeable *tutti* (i.e. everyone playing), or alternatively to a prominent solo or solo group where you can wait for the music to 'catch up'.

Annotated example for Section V J

Tchaikovsky: *Symphony No. 4* (4th movement)

1 Piccolo now written above flute (late 19th century).
2 Flutes 1 and 2 to play in unison.
3 Clarinet in B flat (B is B flat in German, H being B natural), written one tone higher in the key of G rather than F.
4 Bracket embracing woodwind group.
5 Horns in F (2 pairs) written a fifth higher than they sound.
6 2 trumpets in F written a fourth lower than they sound.
7 Tenor trombones written in tenor clef.
8 Bass trombone plays without tuba, indicated by semibreve rest below stave.
9 Timpanist tunes drums to these three notes.
10 Percussion, triangle, cymbals and bass drum written on single lines.

VI Structure and form

A Design in music

1 In music, the word **form** is used both to describe the internal shape and structure of a single movement or piece and also to label the overall plan of a work, e.g. whether it is a suite of dances, a string quartet, or a symphony.

2 Unlike the visual arts which are spatial in conception, music unfolds in time. Nevertheless, as we saw in Chapter II when studying melody, the artistic principles of unity, repetition, contrast, and balance must all be considered when building even the simplest musical structure.

3 These principles apply equally to the shape of a movement and to the plan of a composition as a whole. And it is not only the composer who is aware of these structural elements: the performer and listener too recognize their importance in the way they present or appreciate the piece as a whole.

4 Form is not fixed. It is flexible and is moulded by the composer as he develops his ideas. Certain forms are particularly associated with certain historical periods, e.g. **fugue** in the Baroque era, or **sonata form** in the late 18th century. However, all such forms are subject to evolutionary development, decline, and sometimes resurrection, and there is no 'ideal form' in music.

5 A broad understanding of musical form is best achieved from the study of certain basic structures, which conform to the accepted pattern of a particular form and which may be shown diagrammatically.

B Basic structures

1 Musical structure is dominated by six main forms:

A	**Unitary form:**	in which one idea extends throughout the movement.
AB	**Binary form:**	in which the piece falls into two sections.
ABA	**Ternary form:**	in which the piece has three sections, the first and last identical and enclosing a middle, contrasting, section.

ABACA	**Rondo form:**	an extension of the ternary principle, with a further episode between appearances of the first section.
ABDevAB	**Sonata form:**	a more extended form, related to both binary and ternary. The 'middle section' develops ideas from earlier sections, and is here marked 'Dev'.
ABACABA	**Sonata-rondo form:**	this indicates the reappearance of section B after the middle episode C and the recurrence of section A at points throughout the movement.

2 By the late 17th century, key had an important part to play in structure. With rare exceptions it will be found that:

Section A will be based in the tonic key

Section B will mostly start in or on the dominant (or sometimes the relative major or minor), but where it is the *last* section of a movement (i.e. in binary or sonata structures) it will return in the tonic

Section C will provide a contrast to the tonic and dominant, e.g. the relative minor.

3 A **coda**, or tailpiece, may be added to any of these forms. This may be nothing more than a few extra chords, or else, as in many Beethoven movements, may be of a sufficient scale to balance the development section.

4 Within these six broad structures, there is considerable variation in internal organization. Some of the more common variations are outlined in the following notes. It is desirable to evolve a labelling system which distinguishes melodic content and detail from overall plan. Here Roman numerals are used for the former and capital letters for the main sections. Some analysts use lower-case letters for the melodic content.

5 **Unitary form**

A single idea or figuration carried through the complete piece without sectional divisions. Largely in the tonic key, although modulation may occur in more extended pieces.

A brief coda may be added or, more often, a peroration (summing up) over a tonic pedal, which takes the form of an elaboration of the last chord, lasting sometimes for several bars. Many Bach preludes are in unitary form.

In the sense that they extend a single idea, fugues too may be classed as unitary in form.

Sets of variations may also be said to be unitary, in that they elaborate a single idea – A A¹ A² A³ and so on.

Annotated example

Purcell: *Prelude*

1   Broken chord figuration.
2   Treated sequentially.
3   Broken chord figure inverted.
4   Inverted figure extended on approach to final cadence.
5   Tonic chord arpeggiated.

6   Binary form

A B

Two distinct sections.

Examples date back to the medieval period, but the form became popular in the 17th century for instrumental pieces.

In these, section A sometimes ends on the tonic, but more commonly on the dominant with an imperfect cadence.

B departs from the dominant and then returns to the tonic. Often it contains just a single melodic idea, but the distinction between this and a unitary structure lies in the movement from tonic to dominant and back, and in the two distinct sections.

In later examples, a clear modulation takes place to the dominant and several melodic ideas may be involved. During the B section, several modulations may occur on the way back to the tonic. Both sections are usually repeated, e.g.

A			B		
I	II	III	I	II	III

Examples of this more extended binary form are to be found in the dance suites of Bach and the keyboard sonatas of Domenico Scarlatti.

Annotated example

Handel: *Hornpipe* from *Water Music*

.1   First phrase in tonic.

2   Repeated in sequence a third lower.

3   Then moved upwards for a repeat at a higher pitch.

4   First phrase repeated at original pitch.

5   Rhythmic syncopation arising from long off-beat note across first and second beats.

6   Contrasted melodic movement in jumps leads to

7   Cadence in dominant at end of first section (A).

8   Repeat of first section.

9   Second section continues in dominant.

10   Syncopated idea taken up.

11   Key of D minor (relative of F).

12   Quaver rhythm reversed, stressing first part of each beat.

13   New idea in G minor, compounded of quavers and leaps.

14   Second and third beats of previous bar treated sequentially and given rhythmic thrust by being brought forward on to first and second beats.

15   Climax of section.

16   Ending in tonic.

7   Ternary form

In the *Fitzwilliam Virginal Book* and in other similar collections of the Elizabethan period, many pieces have a three-part structure. These contain three different (but usually related) tunes, each of which is immediately followed by a variation known as a **double** or division.

A   A1   B   B1   C   C1

However, we use the label 'ternary form' more specifically to describe a three-part structure where section A returns after the middle section or **episode**.

A   B   A

Unlike binary form, section A usually ends on the tonic. Where it does not, as in many Haydn examples, it is slightly modified on its return, so that the piece as a whole ends in the tonic key.

Section B is sometimes in the dominant but, as in many Baroque arias, may be a well-contrasted section in the relative minor.

By the middle of the 18th century the form became associated with instrumental music, especially with the minuet. Then each section was repeated as shown below.

A   B   A (= A A B A B A)

Often minuets and other dances were grouped in pairs, and the first dance was played again (customarily without repeats) after the second.

	Minuet I	Minuet II	Minuet I
i.e.	A B A	A B A	A B A

The second minuet was often played by a smaller group with just three instrumental lines and became known as a **trio**.

The **minuet and trio** became a standard movement in larger-scale forms in the 18th century, such as symphonies and string quartets.

In the 19th century, many short piano pieces were in ternary form.

Annotated example

Bach: *Musette* from *Anna Magdalena's Notebook* (BWV Anh. 126)

1   Section A. Largely over D pedal point.
2   Contrasting texture in octaves.
3   First cadence in D.
4   Section B. Motif taken from bar 3.
5   Chromatic movement over dominant pedal in key of A.
6   End of section B echoes end of A.
7   Instruction to repeat section A.

8   **Rondo form**

    | A   B   A   C   A |

The idea of alternating a refrain between solo passages dates back to the early medieval period. The name **rondo** may have come from a round dance, where a recurring burden or refrain was sung by all the dancers as they moved round and several verses or stanzas were sung, perhaps by a soloist, while everybody stood still.

The rondo tune **A** is always in the tonic, while the episodes **B** and **C** may be in related keys. (The number of episodes is not confined to two – there may be more.)

In the late 17th century many harpsichord pieces were in rondo form, and there are many examples in the works of Couperin and Rameau. The recurring tune was sometimes labelled *Rondeau*, and the episodes as '1st couplet', '2nd couplet', and so on.

By the Classical period the rondo was frequently used as a light-hearted finale in a sonata or symphony.

Annotated example

François Couperin: *La Badine* (5th *ordre*)

1   Tune starts on anacrusis which is rhythmically echoed in the start of later phrases.

2   Imperfect cadence ends first phrase, quaver run in left hand links first and second phrases.

3   Second phrase starts like first.

4   Extension of phrase into a six-bar phrase (4 + 2) by means of an interrupted cadence.

5   Rondeau ends in tonic.

6   1st couplet (or episode) reflects some rhythmic and melodic elements of rondeau.

7   New broken-third figure hints at D major, although episode never completely settles in that key.

8   Return to rondeau and on to 2nd couplet.

9   2nd couplet links into rondeau.

10   New melodic figure.

11   Return to downward groups of quavers relate it to rondeau. Again G natural hints at D major.

12   Return to rondeau after repeat of this line.

9 Sonata form

The name refers to the shape of a particular movement, not to the sonata as a whole. To overcome this confusion this form is sometimes called **first movement form** (which is not satisfactory as it can appertain to any movement), or **compound binary form** (which has the merit of underlining the key structure and balance, which derive from binary form). The following diagram will help to make this clear.

A	B

tonic   dominant   dominant   tonic

Simple binary form as found in Corelli, Purcell and other 17th-century composers.

A	B	
I II	I	II

tonic dominant dominant   tonic
                 and other
                 modulations

More extended binary form with two or more melodic units. Found e.g. in Bach suites, Scarlatti sonatas. Move to or from dominant tends to coincide with arrival of II. Usually some sequential modulation at beginning of second section.

Exposition	Development	Recapitulation
I II		I II

tonic dominant dominant   tonic
                 and other
                 modulations

Sonata form with sections renamed. Typical Haydn/ Mozart pattern. Sequential modulations at start of second section extended into a fuller development. Reappearance of I in recapitulation coincides with tonic.

Exposition	Development	Recapitulation	Coda
I II		I II	

tonic dominant dominant   tonic   tonic
                 and other
                 modulations

Increased scale. Sonata movement with lengthy coda added to restore balance following wide-ranging development section. Typical Beethoven plan.

It will be seen that the movement from tonic to dominant and then from dominant back to tonic is a predominant feature of each form. The modulatory treatment of the material at the beginning of the second section **B** is increased until it becomes an important section in its own right called the **development**. To counterbalance the tonal unrest and size of the development a stabilising coda was added, which in later sonatas sometimes acted as a further development, though based round the tonic key rather than round the dominant.

Section **A** of binary form becomes the exposition in sonata form.

The melodic units I and II are generally more clearly defined in character and are termed subjects.

The first subject is always in the tonic key, but the second subject is traditionally in the dominant (see page 197).

(NB In a number of early sonata movements, the first part of the second subject has the same melodic content as the first, but is distinguished by being in the dominant key.)

The first and second subjects are connected by a transition or **bridge passage** which modulates from the tonic to the dominant.

The exposition sometimes has a distinct closing melodic idea in the dominant, which is called a **codetta**, or 'closing thought'.

The exposition is repeated.

Section **B** of binary form becomes in sonata form the **development** and **recapitulation**. In early examples they were repeated as a single section, but this practice gradually died out as their length began to equal that of the repeated exposition.

The **development** takes up material from the exposition and treats it in a variety of ways and keys. It traditionally departs from the dominant and then returns to this key (sometimes over a long dominant pedal) before leading back into the **recapitulation**. The return of the first subject in the tonic key at the beginning of the recapitulation often marks the climax of the movement. The prominence given to this return has given rise to the impression that the movement is actually ternary, rather than binary (a subject of much theoretical discussion).

In the recapitulation the bridge passage *pretends* to modulate, but in fact returns to the tonic key for the second subject group. A **coda** is added to conclude the movement.

Exposition			Development	Recapitulation		Coda
1st	2nd		modulatory,	1st	2nd	Sometimes
Subject	Subject		varied treatment	Subject	Subject	fresh material
(tonic)	Bridge	(dominant)	(dominant-based)	(tonic)	Bridge (tonic)	(tonic-based)

Annotated example

Clementi: *Sonatina Op. 36 No. 2* (1st movement)

(Clementi: *Sonatina Op. 36 No. 2* (1st movement) *cont.*)

Exposition

1 First subject in tonic, G.
2 Transition or bridge passage leading to dominant.
3 Contrasted second subject in D.
4 Repeated with slight embellishment.
5 Codetta or 'closing thought'.

Development

6   First subject material in A minor.
7   Inversion of theme beginning in canon.
8   Third bar semiquaver figure extracted and extended.
9   Semiquaver figure in sequence over dominant pedal, leading to

Recapitulation

10   First subject in tonic.
11   Bridge passage remaining in tonic.
12   Second subject in tonic.
13   Codetta or closing thought now in tonic.
14   Reiterated tonic chord after final cadence as coda.

10   Sonata-rondo form

As its name implies, this is a hybrid, made up of rondo and sonata forms.

From the rondo form it derives the recurring character of A, always in the tonic.

From sonata form it takes its overall scale, the reappearance of the 2nd subject, or episode, in the tonic key and also the modulatory treatment of the middle section.

A	B	A	C	A	B	A	Coda
tonic	dominant	tonic	relative minor, or modulatory	tonic	tonic	tonic	tonic

Towards the end of the Classical period, sonata-rondo form was favoured for the last movements of larger-scale pieces, such as sonatas, symphonies, and concertos.

C   Fugue

A **fugue** is a complex contrapuntal form which reached its peak in the hands of J.S. Bach in the late Baroque period. It is a piece for a number of instrumental parts, or voices, the first of which 'takes flight' (Latin *fuga* = flight), and is followed by the others in an ordered progression. The individual parts share melodic material and weave it into a web of contrapuntal ingenuity. All fugues are different, being free in overall shape though strictly controlled in internal detail. Many divide clearly into three sections, although sometimes the distinction between the second and third sections is blurred.

a **Exposition**. The first voice (which may be either vocal or instrumental) enters with the **subject**, which is generally short and concise. The second voice follows with the **answer**. This is usually on or in the dominant, and is melodically the same as the subject. If it exactly transposes the subject, it is said to be a **real answer**. If it is modified slightly, it is known as a **tonal answer**. Such modification is necessary where the subject features the dominant note prominently: this leads to tonal ambiguity in transposition. In this case, dominant in the subject is answered with tonic, rather than supertonic, which would be a strict note-for-note transposition.

The first voice continues in conjunction with the answer, adding a **countersubject**. Before the third voice enters, the first and second voices may extend their material for a bar or two in the form of a **codetta**.

The third voice enters in the tonic with the subject again, the second voice has the countersubject, and the first voice might either have a second countersubject, or some free counterpoint.

Other voices may subsequently enter if there are more than three parts, or the first voice might add an extra, or **redundant entry**.

Subject	Countersubject	Codetta	Free material	Redundant entry
	Answer	Codetta	Countersubject	Free material
			Subject	Countersubject

b **Middle section**. Here, earlier material derived from the subject or countersubject is introduced in related keys in an episodic and sequential manner, between stricter appearances of the subject or answer. In the episodes the number of voice-parts is often reduced to provide textural variation. This allows the subject to be highlighted on its subsequent reappearance.

c **Final Section**. Here the fugue usually reaches its climax by more frequent entries of the subject, either by overlapping them in a **stretto**, or by piling them up over a pedal point. Devices such as augmentation, diminution and inversion may be found both here and in the middle section.

A **coda** or peroration over a tonic pedal may occur at the end.

Annotated example

Bach: Fugue in C minor from *The Well-tempered Clavier, Book 1*

(Bach: Fugue in C minor from *The Well-tempered Clavier, Book 1. Cont.*)

Exposition

1   Subject in C minor. Motifs ⌐a⌐ and ⌐b⌐ used extensively throughout.
2   Tonal answer pitched on dominant, moving into dominant key of G minor by
    next bar.
3   Countersubject. Semiquaver scale ⌐c⌐ and four-note quaver figure ⌐d⌐ become
    particularly important in middle section.
4   Codetta between answer and next subject entry. Upward scales accompany
    neighbouring-note motif ⌐a⌐.
5   Subject in bass. Countersubject in soprano, alto adds four-note quaver
    figure ⌐d⌐.

Middle section

6   First episode with alternation of motif ⌐a⌐ in soprano and alto accompanied by
    continuous scale passages. Modulates from C minor through B flat towards
7   E flat major for middle section entry of subject (soprano) and countersubject
    (bass).
8   Second episode derived from scale and four-note figure of countersubject.
    Modulates from E flat through F minor to
9   C minor for answer, which moves to G minor as on first appearance.

10 Third episode derived from codetta treatment of scale passage.
11 Further entry of subject in C minor.
12 Fourth episode similar to first –
13 Extended by dialogue between soprano and alto with new material.
14 Final bass entry preceded by run based on dominant.

Final section

15 Subject in bass.
16 Peroration over tonic pedal; subject in soprano with thickened texture.

D   Variation forms

1   As was noted under **ternary form**, a favourite way of extending a piece in the
     16th century was by the immediate repetition of a phrase or section in a varied
     form called a **double** or **division**.

William Byrd: *Wolsey's Wilde*

Continuing repetition of the bass, or the underlying harmony, led to the use of
the term '**Divisions on a Ground**' for this type of piece. The ground basses
were often derived from popular tunes.

2   By the 17th century two dances, the **Passacaglia** and **Chaconne** were mostly
     presented in this fashion as continuous variations over a ground or **basso
     ostinato**, so-called because it obstinately repeated itself over and over again
     throughout the movement. Purcell much favoured using the **ground bass** as a
     structural principle over which he laid the most expressive melodies.

VI D 1 to 5

Purcell: 'When I am laid in earth' from *Dido and Aeneas*

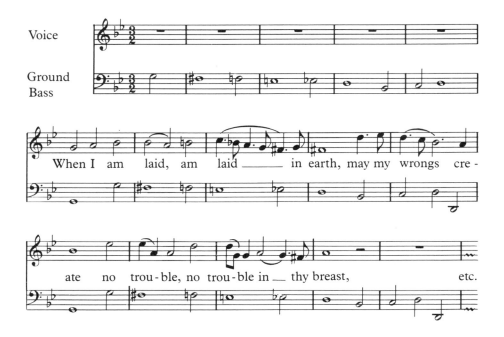

When I am laid, am laid ___ in earth, may my wrongs cre-

ate no trou-ble, no trou-ble in ___ thy breast, etc.

3 Throughout the 18th century and indeed up to Brahms and beyond, composers have written sets of variations, either on an original theme, or on a popular tune of the day, very often taken from a fashionable opera. As with divisions on a ground, in most variations the same harmonic basis is present. If a composition is in a major key, at least one variation will generally be in the minor, and vice versa. The final variation of a set is often extended into a Coda to bring the work to a positive conclusion. In some variation sets this last extended variation is in the form of a fugue, whose subject is derived from the original theme.

Beethoven was a master of variation form. These quotations from his '15 Variations with Fugue on a theme from *Prometheus*', Op. 35, show some of the devices he used.

The theme is in the key of E flat major and has a distinct harmonic bass.

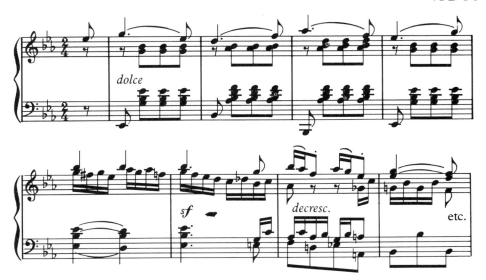

In Variation I the outline of the melody is changed by means of arpeggios and runs, while the harmonic basis is retained intact.

In Variation VI the melody is re-harmonized in C minor.

In Variation VII the theme is treated in canon with the left hand playing the same as the right, only one beat behind.

The outline of the melody is completely broken up in Variation XII.

In Variation XIII the tune disappears, but as usual the harmonic basis is retained.

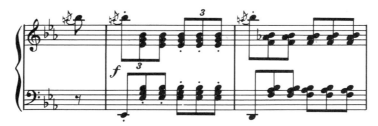

In Variation XV the character of the theme is altered by varying its rhythm and tempo.

And in the Finale the bass of the theme is used as the subject of a fugue.

4 Such techniques are used widely in works which are not otherwise in variation form. A composer will sometimes recapitulate a section, e.g. in a rondo, in varied form.

5 A set of variations may be complete in itself or it may be a single movement in a larger work such as a symphony or string quartet. Haydn wrote many such movements, often with both a major and minor version of the theme, each having two or three variations.

E Longer forms

1 Apart from overtures and tone poems, most larger-scale works are cast in a number of separate movements. These may be related thematically, or may just be complementary in some other way. They will in any case be contrasted in tempo and mood. As with more basic structures, many of these forms are associated with a particular historical period, although some, like the symphony, remained fashionable across a longer time-span.

2 Baroque forms
a Suite (Italian *partita*)
A set of instrumental dances of which the most important in the early 18th century were:
Allemande
German in origin; in $\frac{4}{4}$ time; each phrase usually preceded by one or three semiquavers as an up-beat.

Bach: *Allemande from French Suite No. 1 for harpsichord*

Courante

Two types, the Italian (*corrente*) – a running piece in $\frac{3}{4}$ or the French (*courante*) – a contrapuntal piece in which $\frac{6}{4}$ and $\frac{3}{2}$ metres are mixed, especially at the approach to cadences.

Bach: *Courante* (II) from *English Suite No. 1 in A*

Sarabande

Spanish in origin – slow triple time with a stressed second beat.

Bach: *Sarabande* from *English Suite No. 2 in A minor*

Gigue

A lively piece of British or Irish origin, in compound time. Often treated in fugal style.

Bach: *Gigue* from *French Suite No. 4*

'Optional extras' could be introduced to augment the number of movements and these might include:

Minuet

French in origin, in triple time. Often paired with a second Minuet and treated as ternary form with a repeat.

Handel: *Minuet* from *Harpsichord Pieces*

Bourrée

French in origin. A smooth, easily flowing movement in $\frac{2}{2}$ starting with an upbeat crotchet or pair of quavers.

Bach: *Bourrée* from *French Suite No. 5*

Air

A lyrical contrast to the other dance movements.

Bach: *Air* from *Orchestral Suite No. 3 in D* (BWV 1068)

Gavotte

A lively dance in $\frac{4}{4}$ or $\frac{2}{2}$, with each phrase starting on the half bar. Usually paired with a **musette** to form a trio section. The *musette* takes its name from a French bagpipe and always includes a drone bass.

Bach: *Gavotte* from *English Suite No. 3*

Bach: *Musette* (or *Gavotte 2*) from *English Suite No. 3*

Almost invariably the dances were in binary form.

Each dance in the suite was in the same key, or exceptionally, as in the musette quoted above, in the tonic major or minor.

Suites often opened with a **Prelude** or a **French overture**. This last had a slow first section in dotted rhythm, followed by a quick fugal movement in triple time.

b Trio (Baroque) sonata

Two main types:

i **Sonata da camera** (Chamber sonata), in form just like the basic dance suite.

ii **Sonata da chiesa** (Church sonata), with (usually) four contrasted movements:

1 slow and majestic
2 quick and lively
3 fairly slow and graceful
4 very quick, often a gigue

Such pieces are known as **trio sonatas**, although they customarily involve *four* players: a pair of solo instruments, e.g. two violins or recorders, keyboard (continuo), and cello or viola da gamba (a large bass viol, played like a cello), which doubled the bass line of the continuo part.

Some Baroque sonatas were scored for a single solo instrument with continuo, in which case they were known as 'solo sonatas'.

c Concerto grosso

A concerted piece in which a small group of players (**principale** or **concertino**) alternates with and complements a larger body of players (**tutti** or **ripieno**). As in Bach's 'Brandenburg' concertos, the orchestra or ensemble and concertino group could contain any number or type of instruments. Some concertos resembled *sonate da chiesa* in form, having four contrasted movements. Others, like those of Vivaldi and Bach, have three movements – two quick and a slow middle movement which is often scored for a smaller group of players.

The outside movements generally start with a bold statement for the whole ensemble, which returns between contrasted episodes for the concertino group during the movement. For this reason it is known as a **ritornello** (a little return). Unlike a rondo, however, the ritornello does not always return in complete form, nor invariably in the tonic.

d Cantata

A work for voice(s) and ensemble (from Italian *cantare*, 'to sing'). Of infinite variety in design, but usually containing opening and closing choruses with solo recitatives, arias, and duos in between. Bach wrote a great many sacred cantatas.

3 Classical forms

a Sonata

The name **sonata** is usually associated with a work for one or two players. Works of similar form for larger ensembles are known by the number of players involved, e.g. trio, quartet, quintet, sextet, octet. Further qualification is provided by naming the type of instruments in the score, e.g. string quartet, wind quintet, brass octet. It should be noted that a piano trio is *not* a work for three pianos, but a work for piano with violin and cello.

Symphonies and **sinfoniettas** are orchestral works in the form of a sonata. Most sonatas, string quartets, and symphonies have three or four movements.

The **first movement** is usually lively and in sonata form. It may have a slow introduction.

The **second movement** is slow and may be in almost any of the basic forms, including variations.

The **third movement** (sometimes excluded from the overall structure, especially in solo sonatas) usually acts as light relief after the more serious tone of the first two movements. At first a minuet and trio, becoming in the hands of Haydn a more robust country dance, from Beethoven onwards it develops into a more dynamic scherzo and trio.

Occasionally the slow movement is placed third.

The last movement, or **finale**, is often a rondo or sonata rondo, and is traditionally fast and exhilarating.

b Concerto

A Classical concerto is usually scored for a single instrument with orchestra, instead of a solo group alternating with the **ripieno** (or main body of the orchestra) as in earlier Baroque concertos. The solo part is usually more virtuosic in style than in the earlier type, and the overall structure is similar to the three-movement sonata or symphony of the Classical period although, as always, there are many exceptions.

In a typical concerto of this period the first movement opens with the **exposition** (sometimes termed *ripieno* in this context). It is normally given first to the orchestra *without* the soloist, and with the first and second subject groups both in the tonic key. The soloist then enters, sometimes with new and distinctive material, and joins in a restatement of the exposition with the normal key structure of tonic and dominant for the first and second subjects. After the **development** section, the ensuing **recapitulation** is interrupted towards the end by a sustained $\frac{6}{4}$ chord on the dominant, creating an air of suspense before the start of the soloist's **cadenza** (in which the orchestra remains silent). The cadenza enables the soloist to demonstrate his technical skill; in concertos up to the time of Beethoven he was expected to improvize his own cadenzas, but in later works they were generally written by the composer. (Brahms's Violin Concerto (1878) is one of the last examples of a concerto in which the soloist was required to improvize a cadenza.) A prolonged trill over the dominant chord resolves the opening $\frac{6}{4}$ chord, and signals the re-entry of the orchestra to conclude the movement with a short tutti (with or without the soloist). The second and third movements of a Classical concerto follow similar lines to the corresponding movements of sonatas and symphonies of the same period. The third movement, which is often light and very fast, usually includes a brief cadenza towards the end.

Most of the concertos of Mozart and Beethoven's time, and many of the early Romantic period, adhere roughly to the above plan, although several modifications were gradually introduced. Some works open with a preliminary flourish for the soloist, sometimes brief and sprightly in style, as in Mozart's Piano Concerto No. 9 in E flat, K271, or of a poetic nature, as in Beethoven's Fourth Piano Concerto, or flamboyant, as in his Fifth. In some cases, e.g. the violin concertos of Mendelssohn and Tchaikovsky, movements are linked together by orchestral bridging passages.

4 Romantic forms

During the Romantic period (19th century) the scale of most works was greatly enlarged. Symphonies became more flexible in overall shape, number and order of movements, and key structure. Following Beethoven's example in his Ninth Symphony, several composers, such as Mahler, introduced voices into one or more symphonic movements.

Many musical forms were dictated by extra-musical (e.g. literary or artistic) programmes, e.g. Berlioz's *Symphonie fantastique*. **Programme music** in general became increasingly popular, a fine example being Tchaikovsky's 'fantasy overture' *Romeo and Juliet*. Rhapsodic, freely-structured forms were used more often, although conversely composers also became more interested in the possibilities of unifying a single work by means of thematic relationships between movements. Symphonies of this type include Schumann's Fourth and César Franck's D minor, while Liszt evolved a similar process which he called 'transformation (or metamorphosis) of themes'.

Again following Beethoven's example in his Sixth Symphony (the 'Pastoral'), in which the third, fourth, and fifth movements are played without a break, composers began to link two or more movements together.

The **song-cycle** established itself early in the 19th century with Schubert's great cycles *Die schöne Müllerin* and *Winterreise*; his example was followed by Schumann, Brahms, and Hugo Wolf among others.

Chronology of composers and their works

1 14th and 15th centuries

Machaut, Guillaume de (*c.* 1300–1377) French
A priest and poet as well as composer. Music ranges widely from simple songs (chansons) to highly intricate and expressive polyphonic music.
Lais
Motets
Messe de Nostre Dame (possibly first mass written by a single composer.)
Hoquetus David
Ballades, rondeaux, virelais

Dunstable, John (*c.* 1390–1453) English
A sensitive composer who harnessed the stylistic complexities of the period to his own expressive purposes. Style essentially concordant, unlike much 15th-century polyphony. An internationally famous English composer.
Motets
Masses

Dufay, Guillaume (*c.* 1400–1474) French
A leading composer of his day who held positions in important musical centres in Europe. His music was widely performed, and he influenced many of his contemporaries.
Masses
Motets
Numerous secular works (chansons, etc.)

Josquin des Prés (*c.* 1440–1521) Flemish
Pupil of Ockeghem and one of the finest contrapuntal writers of 15th century. Travelled to Italy where his music was performed and published, with influential results.
Masses (18)
Motets (over 100)
Chansons (over 70, including *El Grillo* (The Cricket))

2 Renaissance

Tallis, Thomas (*c.* 1505–1585) English

One of the great church composers of the period, he set both English and Latin texts. With Byrd and later Morley, held monopoly of printing music and music paper, by order of Queen Elizabeth.
Latin church music
English service music and anthems
Keyboard and consort music

Palestrina, Giovanni (*c*. 1525–1594) Italian
Famed as a composer of sacred unaccompanied vocal music. His highly polished style was greatly admired.
Masses (including *L'homme armé* and *Missa Papae Marcelli*)
Motets
Madrigals (61 sacred and 95 secular)

Byrd, William (1543–1623) English
One of the greatest English composers of all time. His style has the fluency of Palestrina's, but displays an expressive delight in unexpected tonal combinations of a surprising freedom.
Vocal music
  Psalmes, Sonets and Songs of Sadnes and Pietie
  Masses in 3, 4 and 5 parts
  Madrigals
Instrumental music
  Virginal music, especially in *My Ladye Nevell's Booke*, the *Fitzwilliam Virginal Book*, and *Parthenia*

Morley, Thomas (1557–1602) English
Wrote both vocal and instrumental music. Famed for his fine madrigals. His book *A Plaine and Easie Introduction to Practicall Musicke* (1597) was popular for 200 years and is now a valuable source of information about 16th-century music-making.
Church services, anthems and motets
Madrigals, canzonets, etc.
Songs, keyboard and instrumental music

Dowland, John (1563–1626) English
Probably the greatest lutenist composer. Widely known and published.
Vocal music
  The First Booke of Songs and Ayres of Four Partes with Tablature for Lute (1597)
  The Second Booke of Songs and Ayres of 2, 4 and 5 parts (1600)
  The Third and Last Book of Songs and Aires (1603)
Instrumental music
  Lachrymae, or Seaven Teares figured in Seaven passionate Pavans

Lute music
Fantasias and pavans

3   The beginning of opera and oratorio

Monteverdi, Claudio (1567–1643) Italian
His long life spans both the choral polyphonic tradition of the 16th century and
the new *monody* (pieces with a melody line and an accompaniment) of the 17th
century, and his music shows the same qualities of greatness in both.
Operas and ballets
   La favola d'Orfeo
   Il ritorno d'Ulisse in patria
   L'incoronazione di Poppea
   Il ballo delle Ingrate
Religious music
   Motets, *Madrigali spirituali*, masses
Madrigals

Lully, Jean Baptiste (1632–1687) Italian (but spent working life in France)
Associated with court of Louis XIV, famous as the creator of French opera.
Ballets de cour (24)
Comédies-ballets (14, including *Le mariage forcé* and *Le bourgeois gentilhomme*)
Operas (14), including
   Cadmus et Hermione
   Alceste
   Thésée
   Armide
Motets
Instrumental music

Purcell, Henry (1659–1695) English
Perhaps the greatest English composer, he absorbed much from Italian and
French music, but impressed his own character and genius on his works.
Opera and stage works
   Dido and Aeneas
   Dioclesian
   King Arthur
   The Fairy Queen
   The Indian Queen
   The Tempest
Church services and anthems
Choral music
   Festival Odes (25), including *Ode on St. Cecilia's Day*
   Cantatas for solo voices and instruments

Chamber music
  Fantasias, Overtures, Sonatas in 3, 4 and 5 parts
Harpsichord and organ music

4   **17th-century instrumental music**

Corelli, Arcangelo (1653–1713) Italian
Famous as performer, teacher and composer for violin. Output small, but had
great influence on development of trio sonata and concerto.
Five books of Trio Sonatas (12 in each)
12 Concerti grossi, Op. 6

Couperin, François (1668–1733) French
Best known for his harpsichord music which is often programmatic in content.
Wrote an important treatise on harpsichord playing.
Sacred and secular vocal music
Chamber music
Harpsichord music
  Pièces de clavecin (4 books, arranged in *ordres* or suites)
  L'art de toucher le clavecin (treatise)

Vivaldi, Antonio (1678–1741) Italian
A prolific composer, particularly of concertos. Had considerable influence on
Bach.
Chamber music
  60 solo sonatas and 58 trio sonatas
Concertos and Sinfonias
  Over 60 for strings
  Well over 200 for solo violin
  At least 200 others for one or more soloists and orchestra
Masses, oratorios and solo cantatas
Over 40 operas

5   **The Late Baroque – Bach and his contemporaries**

Telemann, Georg Philipp (1681–1767) German
Prolific composer in all forms, but best known now for his instrumental music.
Religious music
  46 Passions
  Oratorios and Masses
Operas
Concertos
  47 for one solo instrument, and 48 others

Chamber music
With and without continuo, including solo and trio sonatas, quartets and
quintets
Keyboard music
Fantasias and 7 suites

Bach, Johann Sebastian (1685–1750) German
Generally considered the greatest master of the late Baroque period. Within the
contrapuntal forms he favoured, his music flows with intense expression.
Church music
Passion according to St Matthew
Passion according to St John
Mass in B minor
Magnificat in D
The Christmas Oratorio
Over 230 church cantatas
Keyboard works and chamber music
Two- and three-part Inventions
French suites
English suites
Partitas
The '48 Preludes and Fugues' (*Das Wohltemperierte Klavier*)
The Art of Fugue
Sonatas for keyboard and violin
Sonatas for keyboard and flute
Concertos for various instruments
6 'Brandenburg' concertos
4 Orchestral Suites
Organ works
Toccatas, preludes and fugues
Sonatas
Preludes on chorales

Handel, Georg Frederic (1685–1759) German (but spent much of working life
in England)
In comparison with Bach, a more worldly, forward-looking composer. His style
is more cosmopolitan, showing German and Italian characteristics skillfully
adapted to the English scene.
Operas
Italian (42), including *Rinaldo*; *Berenice*; *Giulio Cesare*
German (3)

Oratorios and masques (25), including
Acis and Galatea (Masque); *Semele* (English opera-oratorio); *Saul*;
Israel in Egypt; *Messiah*; *Samson*; *Judas Maccabeus*; *Joshua*; *Solomon*; *Jeptha*
Other choral works with orchestra
Alexander's Feast; Settings of the Te Deum (Utrecht, Dettingen, etc.);
Chandos Anthems (11); 4 *Coronation Anthems*
Orchestral works
Water Music; *Music for the Royal Fireworks*; Concertos and concerti grossi;
Overtures
Chamber music
Sonatas (with continuo) for violin, flute, etc.
Trio sonatas for various combinations of instruments
Harpsichord music
Suites, Fugues, Sonatas, etc.
Organ concertos

Scarlatti, Domenico (1685–1757) Italian
During his early career, followed the path of his father Alessandro as a composer
of opera and oratorio. Settled in Lisbon in 1719. From 1728 he lived in Madrid
at the Spanish court, where he wrote over 500 keyboard sonatas.
Operas
Oratorios and cantatas (10)
Keyboard sonatas (555)

6   Some pre-classical composers

Gluck, Christoph Willibald (1714–1787) German
Originally wrote serious operas in the Italian style, and comic ones in French
style, but in later works he moved towards a more realistic style in which the
music was subordinate to the poetry and drama. He stated his principles in the
preface to *Alceste* and his reforms led through Mozart and Weber to the music-
dramas of Wagner.
Operas
Italian (34)
French (19), including
Orfeo
Alceste
Iphigénie en Aulide
Armide
Iphigénie en Tauride

CHRONOLOGY OF COMPOSERS AND THEIR WORKS

Bach, Carl Philipp Emanuel (1714–1788) German
J.S. Bach had several children who were also composers. C. P. E. Bach's sonatas and symphonies are often dramatic works and had considerable influence on the subsequent development of the forms. In his day, he enjoyed more fame than his father.
Solo keyboard (over 200 works)
  Sonatas, variations and fantasias
Concertos
Chamber music
Symphonies (19)
Vocal and choral music
Writings: *Essay on the True Art of Playing Keyboard Instruments*

Bach, Johann Christian (1735–1782) German
Known as the 'young' or 'English' Bach to distinguish him from his elder brother, he worked in London, where Mozart met him in 1764. His style is generally lighter than that of C. P. E. Bach and is typical of the rococo period.
Symphonies
Concertos
Chamber music
Keyboard music
Sacred, dramatic and vocal music

7 The Classical period

Haydn, Joseph (1732–1809) Austrian
His long working life spanned the entire 'Classical' period. He brought forward some traditions of the Baroque, developed in every way the sonata structure and in his later works laid the foundations of musical Romanticism. A spirited, witty, and ingenious composer.
Symphonies
  104 (authenticated), including 12 'London' or 'Salomon' and 6 'Paris' symphonies
Pianoforte sonatas (52)
Chamber music
  83 string quartets, 32 piano trios, 126 baryton trios, etc.
Oratorios
  The Creation
  The Seasons
  The Seven last Words from the Cross (arr. from string quartet)
Operas: originally 20, of which 15 survive

Mozart, Wolfgang Amadeus (1756–1791) Austrian
One of the greatest composers, not only of his age, but of all time. Though born into the rather superficial Rococo period, his genius transformed the conventional idioms of the time into a perfectly balanced and refined Classical style, capable of expressing the deepest emotions.
Symphonies (41), including
　Paris in D (K 297), No. 31
　Haffner in D (K 385), No. 35
　Prague in D (K 504), No. 38
　E flat (K 543), No. 39
　G minor (K 550), No. 40
　Jupiter in C (K 551), No. 41
　(K . . . signifies the order of appearance of the composition in Köchel's chronological catalogue of Mozart's works.)
Operas (20), including
　Idomeneo (opera seria)
　Die Entführung aus dem Serail (Singspiel, or German vernacular opera)
　Le nozze di Figaro (Italian opera buffa)
　Don Giovanni (dramma giocosa)
　Così fan tutte (opera buffa)
　Der Zauberflöte (Singspiel)
Solo instruments with orchestra
　Concertos, etc. for violin (5), violin and viola, piano (27), horn (4), flute (2), flute and harp, oboe, bassoon, clarinet
Church music
　Requiem, Masses and motets
Chamber music
　Piano sonatas (17)
　Sonatas for violin and piano (about 35)
　Piano trios (8); string quartets (23); piano quartets (2)
　Serenades; Divertimentos

Beethoven, Ludwig van (1770–1827) German
Mozart's music seems effortless. Beethoven grappled with his material until he moulded it to his purposes. His thoughts were too powerful to be confined within the Classical style and he expanded its range and structures to encompass the inspiration of his last period.
Symphonies (9)
　No. 1 in C; No. 2 in D; No. 3 in E♭ (*Eroica*); No. 4 in B♭; No. 5 in C minor; No. 6 in F (*Pastoral*); No. 7 in A; No. 8 in F; No. 9 in D minor (*Choral*)

Overtures and incidental music, including
Coriolan
Egmont
Leonora (Nos. 1, 2 and 3)
The Ruins of Athens
Concertos
Piano (5, including the 'Emperor')
Violin Concerto, Triple Concerto for piano, violin, and cello
Chamber music
Septet for strings and wind
17 string quartets, piano trios, etc.
Sonatas for violin and piano
Piano music
32 sonatas
21 sets of variations
Vocal music
Mass in C
Mass in D (*Missa Solemnis*)
Opera
Fidelio

Periods of Composition
First period (Up to about Op. 50, showing the influence of Haydn and Mozart)
Piano sonatas (the 'Pathétique' and the 'Moonlight')
Symphonies Nos. 1 and 2
Piano Concertos Nos. 1 – 3
'Kreutzer' Sonata for violin and piano
Septet for strings and wind
Second period (Op. 50–90 approx.)
Piano sonatas ('Waldstein' (Op. 53) and 'Appassionata' (Op. 57))
Symphonies Nos. 3–8 inclusive
Coriolan and *Egmont* overtures
Opera *Fidelio*
The 'Rasumovsky' Quartets
Piano Concertos Nos. 4 and 5
Third period (Begins roughly with Op. 90)
Piano sonatas (Op. 90, Op. 10, Op. 106 ('Hammerklavier'), Op. 109–111)
Mass in D
Symphony No. 9 in D minor, Op. 125
String Quartets from Op. 127 onwards

8   The beginning of Romanticism

Schubert, Franz (1797–1828) Austrian
Perhaps the first 'Romantic' composer. His structures are classical in origin but he endows them with an expressive lyricism. Especially important as a composer of songs, and all his works are melodic in conception.
Songs (over 600)
Song cycles (3)
   Die schöne Müllerin
   Winterreise
   Schwanengesang (posthumous)
Choral works
   Masses (9)
   Cantatas
Works for the stage
   Rosamunde (Incidental music)
Operas (4)
Chamber music
   Trios, 15 Quartets, Quintets (including 'Trout' Quintet and Quintet in C), Octet
Piano Sonatas (21)
Symphonies (9), including the 'Unfinished'

Weber, Carl Maria von (1786–1826) German
Weber's operas established a German national tradition on which later composers, like Wagner, built.
Operas
   Der Freischütz (The Marksman)
   Preciosa (Incidental music)
   Euryanthe
   Oberon (commissioned for Covent Garden)
Orchestral works, including
   Symphonies, piano concertos and 2 clarinet concertos
Chamber music
Piano music

9   Some 'Romantic' composers

Berlioz, Hector (1803–1869) French

A true Romantic, strongly affected by art and literature. His music is rooted in the Classical idiom, but bursts into the Romantic period on a grand scale.

Operas (3)
 Benvenuto Cellini
 Les Troyens (The Trojans)
 Béatrice et Bénédict
Choral works
 Requiem (*Grand messe des morts*)
 Te Deum
Oratorios
 L'enfance du Christ
 La damnation de Faust
Orchestral works
 Symphonie fantastique (Episodes de la vie d'un artiste)
 Harold en Italie (Symphony with solo viola)
 Roméo et Juliette (Symphony for solo voices, chorus and orchestra)
Overtures (6)
 Le roi Lear
 Le carnaval romain
 Le corsaire, etc.
Writings
 Treatise on Instrumentation
 Memoirs

Mendelssohn-Bartholdy, Felix (1809–1847) German
A composer whose music owes more to the refined and polished Classical idiom than to the free forms and passionate outbursts of Romanticism.
Oratorios
 St Paul
 Elijah
Symphony-Cantata
 The Hymn of Praise (*Lobgesang*)
Overtures
 A Midsummer Night's Dream (with incidental music added later)
 Hebrides (Fingal's Cave)
 Ruy Blas
 Calm Sea and Prosperous Voyage
 The Fair Melusine
Symphonies
 12 early string symphonies
 5 mature symphonies, including the 'Scotch' (No. 3), 'Italian' (No. 4) and 'Reformation' (No. 5)

Concertos
  Violin concerto in E minor
  2 piano concertos
Chamber music
  Piano trios, string quartets, etc.
Piano music
  Songs without words (8 books). Prelude and Fugue in E minor, etc.
Organ sonatas (6)

Schumann, Robert (1810–1856) German
Like Berlioz, deeply affected by Romantic literature. He expressed himself most
lyrically through his songs and keyboard works. Also an influential musical
journalist – drew attention to both Chopin and Brahms.
Piano works
  Abegg Variations (Op. 1)
  Toccata, Sonatas, Romances, etc.
  Sets of pieces, including *Carnaval* and *Davidsbündlertänze*
  Kinderscenen (Scenes from Childhood)
Chamber music
  Piano trios, quartets, piano quintet, etc.
Choral works (with orchestra)
  Paradise and the Peri
Opera
  Genoveva
Symphonies (4)
Songs
  Song cycles: *Dichterliebe* (The Poet's Love), *Liederkreis* (2 sets),
  Frauenliebe und Leben (etc.)
  Numerous single songs
Editorial writings: *Neue Zeitschrift für Musik*

Chopin, Fryderyk (1810–1849) Polish
All Chopin's mature output is for the piano (the favourite Romantic instru-
ment), yet within its limitations his music ranges from tender emotion to power-
ful patriotism and protest.
Ballades and Impromptus
Études
Mazurkas
Nocturnes
Polonaises

Preludes
Waltzes
3 Sonatas
2 Concertos for piano and orchestra

Liszt, Ferencz (1811–1886) Hungarian
Liszt was considered the greatest piano virtuoso of the period, but, unlike
Chopin, he did not confine his writing to the keyboard.
Piano works
    Années de Pèlerinage
    Hungarian rhapsodies
    Études, etc.
    Arrangements and transcriptions
Orchestral works
    Faust Symphony
    Dante Symphony
    Prometheus, Les Préludes, Orpheus and other symphonic poems
Piano concertos (2)
Vocal works
    Masses and oratorios

Wagner, Richard (1813–1883) German
Carried German romantic opera to its highest peak. By writing his own texts
and designing his own productions he aimed to produce a completely unified
'music drama'.
Operas (12)
    Rienzi
    Der fliegende Holländer
    Tannhäuser
    Lohengrin
    Tristan und Isolde
    Die Meistersinger
    The Ring – a trilogy of music dramas with prologue: *Das Rheingold*
    (prologue), *Die Walküre, Siegfried*, and *Götterdämmerung*
    (Twilight of the Gods)
    Parsifal

Verdi, Giuseppe (1813–1901) Italian
Whereas Wagner's operas rely for their impact on a continuous orchestral
setting, Verdi, in true Italian tradition, relied principally on the voice to carry
his message, with flashes of harmonic and orchestral colour to enhance the
dramatic effect.

Operas (28)
- **a** Early, including
  Nabucco; *Ernani*; *Macbeth*
- **b** Middle period, including
  Rigoletto; *Il trovatore*; *La traviata*; *Simon Boccanegra*
- **c** Final period, including
  Don Carlos; *Aida*; *Otello*; *Falstaff*

Choral works
Requiem (in memory of Manzoni)

Bruckner, Anton (1824–1896) Austrian

A church composer and organist who chose to express his deepest feelings through the symphony, in a style related both to Schubert and to Wagner.

Symphonies (10)
No. 0 in D minor; No. 1 in C minor; No. 2 in C minor; No. 3 in D minor; No. 4 in E flat major (Romantic); No. 5 in B flat major; No. 6 in A major; No. 7 in E major; No. 8 in C minor; No. 9 in D minor

Sacred choral music
Masses — No. 1 in D minor; No. 2 in E minor; No. 3 in F minor
Te Deum
Requiem
Motets, etc.

Brahms, Johannes (1833–1897) German

Brahms retained his admiration for Beethoven throughout his life. Consequently he adapted his lyrical and romantic idiom to classical structures which attached great importance to motivic development. Unlike his contemporaries, he wrote no programme music.

Symphonies (4)
No. 1 in C minor; No. 2 in D; No. 3 in F; No. 4 in E minor

Overtures
The 'Tragic'
The 'Academic Festival'

Concertos
For piano (2), violin, violin and cello

Piano sonatas (3)

Variations for piano
– on a theme by Paganini
– on a theme by Haydn
– on a theme by Handel

Songs (over 200)

235

Vocal works
Ein Deutsches Requiem
Schicksalslied
Triumphlied
Gesang der Parzen
Chamber music
Piano trios, quartets, and quintet. String quartets, quintets, and sextets.
Quintet for clarinet and strings, horn trio, etc.

Tchaikovsky, Pyotr Ilich (1840–1893) Russian
Like many Russians, Tchaikovsky was a master of orchestration. His music is
both emotionally highly charged and melodically attractive. While clearly rooted
in a Russian idiom, it is more cosmopolitan in style and outlook than that of his
more avowedly nationalist contemporaries.
Symphonies (6)
No. 1 in G minor (Winter Daydreams); No. 2 in C minor (Little Russian);
No. 3 in D (Polish); No. 4 in F minor; No. 5 in E minor; No. 6 in B minor
(Pathetic)
Concertos
2 for piano, 1 for violin
Overtures
Hamlet
Romeo and Juliet
1812
Symphonic Poem
Francesca da Rimini
Chamber music
String quartets (3)
Piano trio in A minor
Operas (9), including
Eugene Onegin
Mazeppa
The Queen of Spades
Ballets (3)
The Sleeping Beauty
Swan Lake
Nutcracker
Songs (over 100)

10   The Nationalists

Smetana, Bedřich: (1824–1884) Czech

A committed Nationalist composer, his operas and tone poems did much to establish the importance of Czech music.
Operas (7)
The Bartered Bride
Dalibor
Libuše
Orchestral
Má Vlast (My Homeland)
Chamber and piano music
Songs

Borodin, Alexander (1833–1887) Russian
A member of the Russian group of nationalist composers known as 'The Five'. One of the few major amateur composers, being a professor of chemistry by profession.
Opera
Prince Igor (unfinished, completed by Rimsky-Korsakov and Glazunov)
Orchestral
Symphonies (3), including No. 2 in B minor
Tone poem *In the Steppes of Central Asia*
Chamber and piano music

Rimsky-Korsakov, Nikolay (1844–1908) Russian
One of the nationalist group of Russian composers known as 'The Five'. Like Borodin, an essentially amateur composer, being a sailor by profession. Responsible for 'improving' and re-orchestrating several major works by his contemporaries, such as Mussorgsky's *Boris Godunov*. A brilliant orchestrator.
Operas (15)
Snow Maiden
Sadko
The Legend of Tsar Saltan
The Golden Cockerel
Orchestral works
3 symphonies
Spanish Caprice
Sheherazade
Russian Easter Festival Overture

Mussorgsky, Modeste (1839–1881) Russian
A member of 'The Five' Russian nationalist composers. His music is rugged and individual in style. The musical realism displayed in his operas made a considerable impact on many later composers.

Operas and stage works (5)
Boris Godunov
Khovanshchina
Orchestral
Night on the bare mountain
Piano music
Pictures from an Exhibition (orchestrated by Ravel)
Songs, including 3 cycles (*The Nursery*; *Sunless*; *Songs and Dances of Death*)

Dvořák, Antonin (1841–1904) Czech
Like several other 19th-century composers, Dvořák adapted his lyrical impulse to symphonic forms. His style strongly reflects his Czech origins.
Operas (10)
Dimitrij
The Jacobin
The Devil and Kate
Rusalka
Orchestral works
Symphonies (9)
No. 1 in C minor (The Bells of Zlonice); No. 2 in B flat; No. 3 in E flat; No.4 in D minor; No. 5 in F major (formerly No. 3); No. 6 in D (formerly No. 1); No. 7 in D minor (formerly No. 2); No. 8 in C major (formerly No. 4); No. 9 in E minor (*from the New World*, formerly No. 5)
Slavonic Dances
Symphonic variations on an original theme
Overtures
Symphonic poems
Choral works
The Spectre's Bride
Stabat Mater
Chamber music and songs (over 100)

Grieg, Edvard (1843–1907) Norwegian
A master of the short lyric piece, his music shows many Norwegian characteristics coupled with considerable harmonic invention.
Orchestral works
Peer Gynt Suites 1 and 2 (incidental music to Ibsen's play)
Holberg Suite (arranged for string orchestra)
Piano Concerto in A minor
Chamber music
Sonatas: Piano (1); violin and piano (3); cello and piano (1); string quartet

Piano music
Humoresques, *Lyric Pieces*, many 'character pieces'
Songs (over 120)

11 The late Romantics

Puccini, Giacomo (1858–1924) Italian
Essentially an operatic composer, his gift for melody, vivid orchestration and
arresting harmony made him a master of dramatic effect.
Operas (12)
  La Bohème
  Tosca
  Madama Butterfly
  Turandot
Church music; choral and orchestral works; chamber music and songs

Wolf, Hugo (1860–1903) Austrian
His 250 Lieder showed a new realisation of the equality of words and music,
derived from Wagner's music dramas. His works include 6 collections of songs
by a single poet or group of poets including
  53 *Mörike-Lieder*
  51 *Goethe-Lieder*
  20 *Eichendorff-Lieder*
  Spanisches Liederbuch (44 songs)
  Italienisches Liederbuch (46 songs in 2 parts)
Italian Serenade for small orchestra
Opera *Der Corregidor*
String Quartet, piano works and choruses

Mahler, Gustav (1860–1911) Austrian
An important conductor as well as composer. His massive symphonies stretched
symphonic form almost to breaking point. Many include voices.
Symphonies (10)
  No. 1 in D; No. 2 in C minor; No. 3 in D minor; No. 4 in G;
  No. 5 in C sharp minor; No. 6 in A minor; No. 7 in B minor; No. 8 in E flat;
  No. 9 in D; No. 10 in F sharp minor (incomplete)
Vocal works with orchestra
  Das Lied von der Erde
  Das klagende Lied
Songs, including 2 cycles
  Lieder eines fahrenden Gesellen
  Kindertotenlieder

Strauss, Richard (1864–1949) German

His highly dramatic style extended Wagnerian opera almost into the world of Expressionism. Even his non-dramatic music is frequently programmatic in intent. His songs continued the tradition of the German Lied from Schubert through Schumann, Brahms and Wolf.

Operas (15)
  Salome
  Elektra
  Der Rosenkavalier
  Die Frau ohne Schatten
  Arabella
  Capriccio
Songs (over 120)
Symphonies
  Symphonia domestica
  Eine Alpensinfonie
Symphonic poems
  Don Juan
  Death and Transfiguration
  Till Eulenspiegel
  Don Quixote
  Ein Heldenleben

Rakhmaninov, Sergey (1873–1943) Russian

An internationally famous pianist and conductor who composed a considerable number of full-scale works in late romantic idiom.

Symphonies (3)
Piano Concertos (4)
  No. 1 in F sharp minor; No. 2 in C minor; No. 3 in D minor; No. 4 in G minor
  Rhapsody on a theme of Paganini
Keyboard pieces and songs

12   The Parisian scene

Fauré, Gabriel (1845–1924) French

Best known for his Requiem, songs and piano music, all of which display a poetic elegance and at times an adventurous harmonic idiom.

Operas
  Prométhée
  Pénélope
  Masques et bergamasques

Songs and song cycles (including *La bonne chanson*)
Chamber music (including Piano Quartet and Quintet)
Piano music (including Impromptus, Barcarolles and Nocturnes, as well as *Dolly Suite* for piano duet)

Debussy, Claude (1862–1918) French

Debussy admired the music of Wagner but reacted against its German techniques. His music displays certain characteristics similar to the artistic movement known as *impressionism*, but, although atmospheric at times, it displays in its structure and content the traditional French features of clarity and precision. His harmony breaks away from 19th-century progressions and exploits the use of chords in parallel motion.

Orchestral pieces
Prélude à l'après-midi d'un faune
Nocturnes
La Mer
Jeux (ballet)
Opera
Pelléas et Mélisande
Piano music
Suite bergamasque
Children's Corner
Préludes (books 1 and 2)
Images (books 1 and 2)
Études (books 1 and 2)
Songs and chamber music

Satie, Erik (1866–1925) French

His music represents the first complete break with Romanticism in France. Often humorous, it displays in its epigrammatic and highly individual style an experimental quality which points towards the avant-garde.

Stage works
Parade (ballet with scenario by Cocteau and designs by Picasso)
Relâche (ballet)
Piano pieces, including *Gymnopédies* and *Gnossiennes*

Ravel, Maurice (1875–1937) French

Like Debussy, Ravel also shows an underlying Classical approach in his brilliant and evocative style.

Orchestral music
Rhapsodie Espagnole
Le tombeau de Couperin

CHRONOLOGY OF COMPOSERS AND THEIR WORKS

Bolero
2 Piano Concertos (1 for left hand)
Operas (2)
  L'heure espagnole
  L'enfant et les sortilèges
Ballets
  Daphnis et Chloë
  Ma Mère l'oye (also as piano duet)
Chamber music
  String Quartet in F
  Piano Trio
  Sonatas for violin and piano (2)
  Introduction et Allegro for harp, flute, clarinet and string quartet
Piano
  Sonatine; *Jeux d'eau*; *Miroirs*; *Le tombeau de Couperin*; *Gaspard de la nuit*
Songs

Stravinsky, Igor (1882–1971) Russian
Still best known for the barbarism of his early ballets written for Diaghilev's
Ballets Russes. In the 1920s he embraced neo-classicism and finally turned to
quasi-serial techniques. Each of his works has its own unique style.
Ballets
  The Firebird
  Petrushka
  The Rite of Spring
  Les Noces
  Apollo Musagetes
  Agon
Opera
  The Rake's Progress
Choral-orchestral works
  Oedipus Rex (opera-oratorio)
  Symphony of Psalms
  Canticum Sacrum
  Cantata
  Threni
  Requiem Canticles
Orchestral
  Fireworks
  Symphonies of wind instruments
  Symphony in C
  Symphony in 3 movements

Concertos
  Concerto for piano and wind
  Violin concerto
  Ebony Concerto for clarinet
Chamber music
  Octet for wind instruments
  In Memoriam Dylan Thomas for voice, string quartet and 4 trombones
Piano music
Songs

Messiaen, Olivier (b. 1908) French
A religious mystic whose powerful and expressive music has had immense
influence on his younger contemporaries. His music incorporates a great deal of
material derived from bird-song, which is often presented in complex rhythmic
textures which owe much to Oriental music. Also an influential teacher.
Orchestral
  Turangalîla-Symphonie (witness to his Oriental interest)
  Oiseaux exotiques
  Chronochromie
  Couleurs de la cité céleste
Piano
  20 Regards sur l'enfant Jésus
  Catalogue d'oiseaux
Organ
  La Nativité du Seigneur
  Livre d'orgue
Chamber
  Quatuor pour la fin du temps
Vocal
  Cinq rechants
  Poèmes pour Mi (solo voice with orchestra)

13 The English revival

Elgar, Sir Edward (1857–1934) English
Although his techniques and structures are almost wholly German in origin, his
music has an indefinable 'English' quality. He is often rated the first English
composer of stature since Purcell.
Oratorios
  The Dream of Gerontius
  The Apostles
  The Kingdom

Orchestral works
  Enigma Variations
  Concert overture: *Cockaigne*
  Symphonic poem: *Falstaff*
  Symphonies (No. 1 in A flat, No. 2 in E flat)
Concertos
  Violin concerto in B minor; Cello concerto in E minor
Chamber music
  String quartet
  Piano quintet

Delius, Frederick (1862–1934) English
Delius's music has a more rhapsodic and nostalgic quality than Elgar's. It shows a combination of German, French and, through its folk-like tunes, English features.
Orchestral
  Paris: the song of a great city
  On hearing the first cuckoo in Spring
  Brigg Fair: an English rhapsody
  Dance Rhapsody (1 and 2)
  Appalachia
Concertos: piano, violin, cello
Operas (6)
  Koanga
  A Village Romeo and Juliet
Choral-orchestral works (8)
  Sea Drift
  A Mass of Life

Vaughan Williams, Ralph (1872–1958) English
His idiom was shaped by early English church music and folk-song, but works like the 4th and 6th Symphonies strike a more jarring note.
Symphonies (9)
  A Sea Symphony (chorus and orchestra) (No. 1)
  A London Symphony (No. 2)
  Pastoral Symphony (No. 3)
  Symphony No. 4 in F minor; No. 5 in D; No. 6 in E minor; No. 7 in D minor (*Sinfonia Antartica*); No. 8 in D minor; No. 9 in E minor
Orchestral
  The Wasps (incidental music to Aristophanes' comedy)
  Fantasia on a theme by Tallis for double string orchestra
  Concerto grosso for strings

Solo instruments and orchestra
  The Lark Ascending (violin and orchestra)
  Concerto Accademico (violin and strings)
  Flos Campi (viola, choir and orchestra)
  Concertos: oboe and strings; 2 pianos
Choral works
  Towards the Unknown Region
  Five Mystical Songs (baritone, chorus and orchestra)
  Sancta Civitas (oratorio)
  Benedicite
  Dona nobis pacem
  Five Tudor Portraits
  Hodie
Chamber music
  2 string quartets
  Preludes on Welsh hymn tunes (household music) for strings
Song cycles
  On Wenlock Edge (Housman)
Songs and folk-songs (with piano accompaniment)

Holst, Gustav (1874–1934) English
His broad, lively mind was reflected in the originality of much of his music.
Closely associated with Vaughan Williams and the English folk-song revival, his
style is nevertheless eclectic.
Operas
  Savitri
  The Perfect Fool
  At the Boar's Head
Choral-orchestral
  3 Choral Hymns from the Rig Veda
  The Hymn of Jesus
  A Choral Fantasia
Orchestral
  Suites Nos. 1 and 2 for military band
  St Paul's Suite
  The Planets
  A Fugal Overture
  Egdon Heath

Ireland, John (1879–1962) English
A composer who is probably at his best in small-scale forms such as lyrical
pieces for piano, and songs.

Orchestral
  Prelude: The Forgotten Rite
  Mai–Dun: symphonic rhapsody
  A London Overture
  Piano Concerto
Chamber music
  Piano trios
  Sonatas for violin and piano (2)
  Fantasy-Sonata for clarinet and piano
Choral
  These Things Shall Be
  Morning and evening services
Piano pieces and songs

Bax, Sir Arnold (1883–1953) English
From 1942 he was Master of the King's Musick. His orchestral works have a highly-coloured idiom which is used for expressive ends rather than for pure display.
Orchestral works
  Symphonies (7)
  Overture to a Picaresque Comedy
  Symphonic poems: *November Woods*; *The Garden of Fand*; *Tintagel*
  Symphonic variations for piano and orchestra
  Concertos for violin; cello
Choral music
  Enchanted Summer
  Mater ora filium and other unaccompanied motets
Chamber music
  Elegiac Trio; quintet for harp and strings
  String quartets; piano quartet and quintet
  Sonatas for violin and piano (3); viola and piano, clarinet, cello
  Nonet
  Piano sonatas (4) and sonata for 2 pianos
Songs: folk-song arrangements

Bliss, Sir Arthur (1891–1975) English
Master of the Queen's Musick from 1953, his music was in the early part of his career very forward-looking. He is probably best remembered for *Checkmate* and his other ballets.
Stage works
  Checkmate (ballet)
  Miracle in the Gorbals (ballet)

Adam Zero (ballet)
The Olympians (opera)
Film scores
  Things to Come
  Conquest of the Air
Orchestral
  Colour Symphony
  Piano Concerto
Choral-orchestral
  Morning Heroes
  Pastoral
Vocal and chamber music

14   Germany in the 20th century

Schoenberg, Arnold (1874–1951) Austrian
A direct musical descendant of Wagner, Liszt and Strauss, he turned early to an atonal idiom as an aid to his expressionist aims. From there he developed a systematic 12-note (serial) technique which had a profound effect on the subsequent evolution of 20th-century music.
Operas (4)
  Erwartung
  Moses und Aron
Orchestral
  Pelleas und Melisande (symphonic poem)
  5 *Orchesterstücke*
  2 chamber symphonies
Choral works
  Gurrelieder (Songs of Gurra) with orchestra
  Friede auf Erden (unaccompanied chorus)
  Die Jacobsleiter (oratorio)
Voice with orchestra
  Songs (Op. 8, Op. 22)
  Pierrot Lunaire – cycle of 21 songs
Songs with piano
Chamber music
  String quartets (4); string sextet *Verklärte Nacht*
  Serenade, Op. 24
  Suite, Op. 29
Piano music
  3 Pieces, Op. 11; Suite, Op. 25; 5 Pieces, Op. 23
Treatises: on harmony, composition, counterpoint

CHRONOLOGY OF COMPOSERS AND THEIR WORKS

Webern, Anton (1883-1945) Austrian
A master of concision, many of his pieces last only a minute or so. Every single note has a vital role to play in the texture of his music. Like his teacher Schoenberg, he moved from atonalism to serialism.
Orchestral
  Passacaglia, Op. 1 for full orchestra
  6 Pieces, Op. 4
  5 Pieces, Op. 10
  Symphony, Op. 21 for clarinets, 2 horns, harp and strings
  Variations, Op. 30
Choral works
  Das Augenlicht (cantata), Op. 26 for chorus and orchestra
  Cantatas (2) for solo voice(s), chorus and orchestra, Opp. 29 and 31
Chamber music
  5 *Movements*, for string quartet
  6 *Bagatelles*, for string quartet
  String trio (violin, viola and cello)
  Quartet, Op. 22 for violin, clarinet, tenor saxophone and piano
  String quartet, Op. 28
Piano
  Variations, Op. 27
Pieces for: violin and piano (4); cello and piano (3)
Songs

Berg, Alban (1885-1935) Austrian
A more immediately expressive composer than Webern, he worked on a larger scale. Also a pupil of Schoenberg, but his use of serial techniques was less strictly applied than Webern's. Best remembered for his operas.
Operas
  Wozzeck
  Lulu
Works with orchestra
  Concerto for violin and orchestra (To the memory of an angel)
  7 *Early Songs*
  5 *Altenberglieder*
  Der Wein (concert aria for soprano and orchestra)
Chamber music
  Chamber Concerto for piano, violin and 14 wind instruments
  Lyric Suite for string quartet
Songs

248

Hindemith, Paul (1895–1963) German

Hindemith composed extensively in all forms and apart from a few very early works his music is lyrical and tonally-based. He is associated with the *Gebrauchsmusik* (utility music) movement of the 1920s, his aim being to make his music both useful and playable by amateurs. His book *The Craft of Musical Composition*, written in the late 1930s, reflects his teaching and his theory of expanded tonality. He was a first-rate viola-player, giving the first performance of Walton's Viola Concerto.

Operas (9)
   Mathis der Maler
   Die Harmonie der Welt
Ballets (4)
   Nobilissima Visione
Orchestral works include
   Symphonic Metamorphosis of Themes by Carl Maria von Weber
   Concertos for many solo instruments
Chamber music and keyboard music
Songs and many works for children
Books include
   The Craft of Musical Composition
   A Composer's World: Horizons and Limitations

Stockhausen, Karlheinz (b. 1928) German

His music is structurally diverse. He has shown great interest in the possibilities of using electronics, and many of his works employ large forces both live and taped.

Kontra-Punkte (ensemble)
Klavierstücke I-IV, V-X and XI
Gruppen for three orchestras
Zyklus for percussion
Kontakte for piano, percussion and electronic sounds
Momente for voices and 13 instruments
Mikrophonie I for tam-tam and electronics
Stimmung for 6 singers

15 20th-century Scandinavian composers

Nielsen, Carl (1865–1931) Danish

His music grew from earlier European and Scandinavian traditions and displayed an extended range of chromatic harmony, though still rooted in the tonal system. He showed a preference for contrapuntal textures and cyclic forms.

Operas, stage works and incidental music
Choral works
  Cantatas, motets, etc.
Orchestral works
  Little Suite for strings
  Helios Overture
  Symphonies (6), includings No. 4 (*The Inextinguishable*)
Concertos for violin, flute, clarinet
Chamber music
  String quartets (4)
  Quintet for wind instruments
  Sonatas for violin and piano
  Pieces for oboe and piano, clarinet and piano, solo piano and organ
Songs

Sibelius, Jean (1865–1957) Finnish
A 20th-century symphonic composer whose roots lie in the music of
Tchaikovsky and Brahms. His idiom is, however, highly individual, a blend of
richness and austerity. He grappled with the structural problems of building up
complex structures, such as a symphony, from tiny fragments of melody.
Orchestral works
  Symphonies (7) (8th unfinished)
  Overtures: *Karelia*
  Tone-poems: *En Saga*; *Finlandia*
  Legends: *Lemminkäinen* (including *The Swan of Tuonela*)
  Symphonic poems: *Tapiola*; *The Oceanides*
Choral works with orchestra, with organ, and unaccompanied
Solo instrument with orchestra
  Violin concerto in D minor
Chamber music
  String quartet in D minor (*Voces Intimae*)
  Sonatas for violin and piano, and for cello and piano
  Numerous pieces for piano
Songs, and a song cycle

16 Composers of Eastern Europe

Janáček, Leoš (1854–1928) Czech
Best known for his nationalistic operas which display a powerful, sinewy but
expressive idiom. His word-setting faithfully reflects the speech patterns of his
native language.

Operas (9)
   Jenůfa
   Kat'á Kabanová
   The Cunning Little Vixen
   The Makropulos Affair
   From the House of the Dead
Orchestral
   Taras Bulba
   Sinfonietta
Chamber music
   Violin sonata
   String quartets (2)
Vocal and choral music
   Glagolitic Mass

Bartók, Béla (1881–1945) Hungarian
His music is strongly Hungarian in rhythmic and melodic detail. The middle-period works, like so much music of the 1920s, are angry and strident, while the later works, though still infused with Bartók's characteristic vitality, are more approachable in their almost wistful mellowness.
Stage works
   Duke Bluebeard's Castle (opera)
   The Wooden Prince (ballet)
   The Miraculous Mandarin (ballet)
Orchestral works
   Divertimento for strings
   Dance Suite
   Music for strings, percussion and celesta
   Concerto for orchestra
Solo instruments and orchestra
   Concertos: piano (3); violin (2); viola
   Rhapsodies for violin and orchestra (2)
   Rhapsody for piano and orchestra
Choral music
   Cantata Profana, for solo voices, choir and orchestra
Chamber music
   String quartets (6); violin and piano sonatas (2)
   Piano sonata and sonatina
   Sonata for 2 pianos and percussion
   Sonata for unaccompanied violin

Piano music
  Mikrokosmos (153 progressive pieces)
  Bagatelles
  Burlesques
  Allegro barbaro
Songs – extensive collections, and many arrangements of Hungarian,
Slovak and Rumanian folk-songs

Lutoslawski, Witold (b. 1913) Polish
His early music shows the influence of Bartók. He is one of several modern
composers who have explored the possibilities of rhythmic and tonal indeter-
minacy (aleatory techniques).
Orchestral
  Concerto for Orchestra
  Funeral Music (in memory of Bartók)
  Symphonies (2)
  Livre pour orchestre
  Venetian Games
  Cello concerto
  Mi-parti
Choral-orchestral
  Paroles tissées

17 Two Russians

Prokofiev, Sergey (1891–1953) Russian
His music is direct in its emotional appeal, often playful and satirical. Though
characteristically Russian in style, the effect of his European sojourns is not
difficult to trace, especially the influence of Ravel. Favours classical structures.
Operas (8)
  Love for Three Oranges
  War and Peace
  The Duenna
  The Prodigal Son
Ballets (7)
  Romeo and Juliet
  Cinderella
Orchestral works
  Symphonies (7)
  Scythian Suite
  Russian Overture
  Egyptian Nights (suite – incidental music to Shakespeare and Shaw)

Peter and the Wolf, for narrator and orchestra
Concertos: piano (5) – 1 for left hand; violin (2); cello (1)
Chamber music
Songs and piano pieces, including 8 piano sonatas

Shostakovich, Dmitry (1906–1975) Russian
His 15 symphonies, which span his entire composing career, are central to his output, as are his 15 string quartets. His music has an impressive expansiveness and has the power to move the listener by virtue of its expression of conflicting emotions – pathos and anger are contrasted with more confident, life-affirming music.
Operas (4)
  The Nose
  The Lady Macbeth of the Mtsensk District
The Gamblers
Ballets (4)
  The Age of Gold
Incidental music to plays including Shakespeare's *Hamlet*, *King Lear* and *Othello*
Film music
Symphonies (15)
Concertos: piano (2); violin (2); cello (2)
Chamber music
  String quartets (15)
  2 Piano trios, and Piano Quintet
  Sonata for cello and piano
Piano
  Sonatas
  24 Preludes and Fugues
  Numerous piano pieces
Songs

18 Some 20th-century Americans

Ives, Charles (1874–1954) American
His forward-looking, unconventional music (which often quotes freely from a wide range of other music) at first baffled the public, but in time contributed much to the development of 20th-century compositional techniques.
Orchestral and band
  Symphonies (4)
  Orchestral Set No. 1 (3 Places in New England)
  Central Park in the Dark
  Tone roads No. 1

Chamber music
  Violin sonatas (4)
  String quartets (2)
  Piano trio
Keyboard works, including the Sonata No. 2(*Concord, Mass.*)
Choral and vocal music

Copland, Aaron (b. 1900) American
Well known for his popular works like *El salón México* and *Billy the Kid*, which
have a distinct American flavour. Much of his music is of sterner cast, and
typically displays an intricate interplay of cross-rhythms.
Opera
  The Tender Land
Ballets, film and incidental music
  Billy the Kid (ballet)
  Appalachian Spring (ballet)
Orchestral works
  Symphonies (3) including *A Dance Symphony*
  El salón México
  Symphonic Ode
  Connotations
  Music for a Great City
  Inscape
Concertos: piano and orchestra; clarinet and orchestra
Speaker and orchestra
  A Lincoln Portrait
Chamber music
  Vitebsk (Piano Trio)
  2 *Pieces* for string quartet
  Nonet for strings
  Sonata for violin and piano
  Threnody I: Igor Stravinsky, in memoriam
Piano
  Sonata
  Passacaglia
  Danzan Cuban for 2 pianos
  Night thoughts (*Homage to Ives*)

Cage, John (b. 1912) American
An experimental composer, greatly interested in indeterminacy, novel sound
effects, noise, silence, and Oriental philosophy. He has, through his music and

writings, inspired a fresh appraisal of the basis of composition and a fresh approach to listening.

Construction in Metal, for percussion sextet
Imaginary Landscapes (5) for percussion and electronics
Fontana Mix, for tape
4'33" (the notorious piece which is entirely silent)
Music of Changes, for piano
Atlas Eclipticalis, for orchestra
Water Music, for tape
HPSCHD, for 7 harpsichord soloists and 51 tape machines
Writings
    Silence; *A year from Monday*

19 England in the 20th century

Walton, Sir William (1902–1983) English
Not a prolific composer, but most of his works have found a place in the permanent repertoire. At times witty and brilliant, at others lyrical and dramatic, his style is characterised by rhythmic energy.

Operas
    Troilus and Cressida
    The Bear
Entertainment
    Façade, for reciter and instrumental ensemble
Orchestral
    Symphonies (2)
    Overtures: *Portsmouth Point*; *Scapino*; *Johannesburg Festival Overture*
    Marches: *Crown Imperial*; *Orb and Sceptre*
    Variations on a theme by Hindemith
    Improvisations on an Impromptu of Benjamin Britten
    Concertos for violin, viola and cello
Chamber music
    String quartets (2); Sonata for violin and piano

Tippett, Sir Michael (b. 1905) English
A thoughtful composer-philosopher whose complex but moving music derives from such diverse elements as Purcell and jazz.

Operas
    The Midsummer Marriage
    King Priam
    The Knot Garden
    The Ice Break

Orchestral
   Symphonies (4)
   Concerto for double string orchestra
   Piano Concerto
   Concerto for Orchestra
   Fantasia concertante on a theme of Corelli, for strings
   Triple Concerto
Chamber music
   Piano sonatas (3)
   String quartets (4)
Choral
   A Child of our Time (oratorio)
   The Vision of St Augustine (oratorio)
Writings
   Moving into Aquarius; *Music of the Angels*

Britten, Benjamin (Lord Britten) (1913–1976) English
Almost certainly at his best when writing for voices, whether solo, choral or operatic. His direct and vivid style made him a fine operatic composer.
Operas
   Peter Grimes
   The Rape of Lucretia
   Albert Herring
   Let's make an Opera
   Gloriana
   Billy Budd
   The Turn of the Screw
   Noye's Fludde
   A Midsummer Night's Dream
   Owen Wingrave
   Death in Venice
Church Parables
   Curlew River
   The Burning Fiery Furnace
   The Prodigal Son
Choral
   A Boy was Born
   A Ceremony of Carols
   St Nicholas
   Rejoice in the Lamb
   Spring Symphony

Cantata Academica
War Requiem
Orchestral
  Variations on a theme of Frank Bridge for strings
  Sinfonia da Requiem
  Cello Symphony
  Young Person's Guide to the Orchestra (Variations and Fugue on a theme of
  Purcell)
Chamber music
  String quartets (3)
  Cello suites (3); cello sonata
  6 *Metamorphoses after Ovid* for oboe
Song cycles (with orchestra or piano)
  Les Illuminations (Rimbaud)
  Seven sonnets of Michelangelo
  Serenade for tenor, horn and strings
  Nocturne
  A Charm of Lullabies
  Winter Words
  Canticles (5)

Birtwistle, Harrison (b. 1934) English
Not a prolific composer, but a considerable number of his works have been
widely performed. Like Maxwell Davies he was a student at Manchester. His
music is distinguished by its poetic feeling and dramatic presentation.
Opera
  Punch and Judy
Cantatas
  Down by the Greenwood Side
Orchestral works include
  The Triumph of Time
  Silbury Air
  Melancolia I
  Earth Dances
Instrumental and vocal works
  Refrains and Choruses (without voices)
  Tragoedia (without voices)
  Verses for ensembles (without voices)
  The Fields of Sorrow
Brass band
  Grimethorpe Aria

Maxwell Davies, Peter (b. 1934) English
Studied at Royal Manchester College of Music with Richard Hall. His music
draws inspiration from sources as wide as medieval music, the fox-trot and the
landscape of the Orkneys. He has written a considerable number of works
which involve the players in a semi-dramatic presentation, a genre which has
been termed 'music-theatre'. Formed *The Fires of London* in 1970 and has
written many works for them.
Operas (4)
　Taverner
　The Martyrdom of St Magnus
Theatre pieces include
　Eight songs for a Mad King
Vocal and orchestral (or chamber ensemble)
　O magnum mysterium
　Revelation and Fall
　Hymn to St Magnus
Orchestral
　1st Fantasia on In Nomine of John Taverner
　St Thomas' Wake
　Worldes Blis
　Symphonies (3)
　Violin concerto

Bennett, Richard Rodney (b. 1936) English
His music shows traditional, atonal and jazz influences and has wide appeal. He
has written over 35 film scores and, in addition to composing, is a fine pianist in
both classical and jazz idioms.
Operas (4)
　The Mines of Sulphur
　Victory
Orchestral works
　Symphonies (2)
　Concerto for Orchestra
　Commedia III for 10 instruments
　Music for Strings
　Concertos for piano and for several other instruments
Vocal, chamber and piano music

Comparative Chronology

Composers	Poets and writers	Artists and architects
	Dante (It.) 1265-1321	Giotto (It.) 1276-1336
Machaut (Fr.) 1300-1377	Petrarch (It.) 1304-74	
	Chaucer (Eng.) c. 1340-1400	Brunelleschi (It.) 1337-1446
Dunstable (Eng.) 1390-1453		Van Eyck (Flemish) 1385-1441
		Donatello (It.) 1386-1466
Dufay (Fr.) 1400-1474		
		Bellini (It.) 1426-1516
Josquin Desprès (Flemish)		Botticelli (It.) 1444-1510
1445-1521		Bramante (It.) 1444-1514
	Skelton (Eng.) c.1460-1529	Leonardo da Vinci (It.)
Jannequin (Fr.) c. 1475-c. 1560	More (Eng.) 1478-1535	1452-1519
		Dürer (Ger.) 1471-1528
		Michelangelo (It.) 1475-1564
	Rabelais (Fr.) 1494-1553	Titian (It.) c. 1487-1576
Tallis (Eng.) 1505-85		Holbein (Ger.) 1497-1543
		Cellini (It.) 1500-71
		Palladio (It.) 1508-80
Andrea Gabrieli (It.) 1520-94		Tintoretto (It.) 1518-94
Palestrina (It.) 1526-94		Bruegel (Flemish) 1525-69
Byrd (Eng.) 1543-1623	Cervantes (Sp.) 1547-1616	Hilliard (Eng.) 1547-1619
Morley (Eng.) 1557-1602	Spenser (Eng.) 1552-99	
Giovanni Gabrieli (It.)		
1557-1612		
Dowland (Eng.) 1563-1626	Marlowe (Eng.) 1564-93	
	Shakespeare (Eng.) 1564-1616	
Monteverdi (It.) 1568-1643	Jonson (Eng.) 1573-1637	Inigo Jones (Eng.) 1573-1641
	Donne (Eng.) 1573-1631	Caravaggio (It.) 1573-1610
Schütz (Ger.) 1585-1672		Poussin (Fr.) 1594-1665
		VanDyck (Flemish) 1599-1641
		Velasquez (Sp.) 1599-1660
		Borromini (It.) 1599-1667
	Milton (Eng.) 1608-1674	Rembrandt (Dutch) 1606-69
	Molière (Fr.) 1622-73	
	Bunyan (Eng.) 1628-88	
Lully (It./Fr.) 1632-87	Dryden (Eng.) 1631-1700	Wren (Eng.) 1630-1723
	Pepys (Eng.) 1633-1703	Vermeer (Dutch) 1632-1675
	Racine (Fr.) 1635-99	
Corelli (It.) 1653-1713		Hardoluin-Mansart (Fr.)
Purcell (Eng.) 1659-95		1646-1708

Compositions, books, plays, buildings and works of Art	Some other significant people and events
Rheims Cathedral begun 1211 Salisbury Cathedral 1220-65	Magna Carta 1215
Dante began *Divine Comedy* 1300	Papal court at Avignon 1309
Chaucer began *Canterbury Tales* 1387	
Guildhall (London) built 1411-46	Battle of Agincourt 1415
King's College, Cambridge 1446-1515	
	Caxton starts press at Westminster 1476
Da Vinci painted *Last Supper* 1495-7	First printed music by Petrucci in Venice 1509 Henry VIII came to throne 1509
Jannequin's Chanson *La Guerre*, 1529	Henry VIII summoned 'Reformation Parliament' 1529
English Book of Common Prayer 1549 Palestrina wrote *Missa Papae Marcelli* in honour of Pope Marcellus 1555	Monasteries suppressed 1538
Palladio's *Treatise on Architecture* 1570	Drake sails round world 1577-80
Monteverdi's first madrigal book 1587 Spenser writes *Faerie Queen* 1590-6 Morley's *Plaine and Easie Introduction* 1597 Shakespeare's *Hamlet* 1600 *The Triumphs of Oriana* 1601 Cervantes started *Don Quixote* 1605 Monteverdi produced *Orfeo* 1607	Oliver Cromwell 1599-1658 Death of Elizabeth I 1603
	Civil War in England 1642-49 Louis XIV reigned 1643-1715
Pepys begins his diaries 1659	

COMPARATIVE CHRONOLOGY

Composers	Poets and writers	Artists and architects
		Hawksmoor (Eng.) 1661-1736
Couperin (Fr.) 1668-1733	Congreve (Eng.) 1670-1729	
Vivaldi (It.) 1678-1741		
Telemann (Ger.) 1681-1767		
Rameau (Fr.) 1683-1764		
Domenico Scarlatti (It.) 1685-1757		
J.S. Bach (Ger.) 1685-1750		
Handel (Ger.) 1685-1759	Pope (Eng.) 1688-1744	Neumann (Ger.) 1687-1753
	Voltaire (Fr.) 1694-1778	Hogarth (Eng.) 1697-1764
		Canaletto (It.) 1697-1768
Boyce (Eng.) 1710-79	Fielding (Eng.) 1707-54	
	Rousseau (Fr.) 1712-1778	
C.P.E. Bach (Ger.) 1714-88	Sterne (Eng.) 1713-68	
Gluck (Ger.) 1714-87	Diderot (Fr.) 1713-84	
	Gray (Eng.) 1716-71	
	Smollett (Eng.) 1721-71	Stubbs (Eng.) 1724-1806
	Burney (Eng.) 1726-1814	Gainsborough (Eng.) 1727-88
Haydn (Ger.) 1732-1809	Beaumarchais (Fr.) 1732-99	R. Adam (Scot.) 1728-92
J C Bach (Ger.) 1735-82		
	Goethe (Ger.) 1749-1832	Goya (Sp.) 1746-1828
Clementi (It.) 1752-1832	Sheridan (Eng.) 1751-1816	
Mozart (Austr.) 1756-1791	Blake (Eng.) 1757-1827	
		Nash (Eng.) 1762-1835
Beethoven (Ger.) 1770-1827	Wordsworth (Eng.) 1770-1850	
	Jane Austen (Eng.) 1775-1817	Turner (Eng.) 1775-1851
	E.T.A. Hoffmann (Ger.) 1776-1822	Constable (Eng.) 1776-1837
Field (Irish) 1782-1837		Ingres (Fr.) 1780-1867
Weber (Ger.) 1786-1826	Byron (Eng.) 1788-1824	
	Keats (Eng.) 1791-1821	
	Shelley (Eng.) 1792-1822	Charles Barry (Eng.) 1795-1860
Schubert (Austr.) 1797-1828	Heine (Ger.) 1797-1856	Delacroix (Fr.) 1798-1863
	Balzac (Fr.) 1799-1850	
	Pushkin (Russ.) 1799-1837	
Glinka (Russ.) 1803-57	Victor Hugo (Fr.) 1802-85	Paxton (Eng.) 1801-65

COMPARATIVE CHRONOLOGY

Compositions, books, plays, buildings and works of Art	Some other significant people and events
	Charles II returned to throne from exile in France 1660
Molière wrote *Le bourgeois gentilhomme* 1670	Plague and Fire of London 1665-6
St. Paul's cathedral rebuilt by Wren 1675-1710	
Enlargement of Versailles completed 1678	
Purcell's *Dido and Aeneas* 1679	
	1st piano built by Cristofori 1709
Couperin's *L'art de toucher le clavecin* 1716	
Swift's *Gulliver's Travels* 1726	
The Beggar's Opera 1728	
Bach composed *B minor Mass* 1731-8	
Hogarth's *Rake's Progress* 1735	Frederick the Great reigned 1740-86
Handel's *Messiah* in Dublin 1742	
Neumann's pilgrimage church of Vierzehnheiligen begun 1743	
Fielding's *Tom Jones* 1749	Holywell Music Room, Oxford, opened 1748
Hogarth's *Gin Lane* 1751	Diderot and d'Alembert's *Encyclopédie* published 1751
	British Museum founded 1753
	Voltaire's *Dictionary of Philosophy* 1764
	Napoleon Bonaparte 1769-1821
Burney's *History of Music* 1776	American Declaration of Independence 1776
	Adam Smith's *Wealth of Nations* 1776
Beaumarchais' play *Le mariage de Figaro* 1784	
Mozart's *Marriage of Figaro* 1785	
Blake's *Songs of Innocence* 1789	Bank of England started 1788
Haydn's symphonies Nos. 93-104 composed for London 1791-5	French Revolution begins 1789
Haydn's *Creation*, Vienna 1798	
Beethoven's *Eroica* symphony 1804	Napoleon declares himself Emperor 1804

COMPARATIVE CHRONOLOGY

Composers	Poets and writers	Artists and architects
Berlioz (Fr.) 1803-69	George Sand (Fr.) 1804-76	
Mendelssohn (Ger.) 1809-47	Edgar Allan Poe (Amer.)	
Chopin (Polish) 1810-49	1809-49	
Schumann (Ger.) 1810-56	Tennyson (Eng.) 1809-1892	
Liszt (Hung.) 1811-86	Dickens (Eng.) 1812-70	
Wagner (Ger.) 1813-83	Emily Brontë (Eng.) 1814-48	
Verdi (It.) 1813-1901	Charlotte Brontë (Eng.) 1816-55	
	Whitman (Amer.) 1819-92	
	George Eliot (Eng.) 1819-80	
	Baudelaire (Fr.) 1821-67	
Franck (Fr.) 1822-90	Dostoevsky (Russ.) 1821-81	
Smetana (Czech) 1824-84		
Bruckner (Austr.) 1824-96		
	Tolstoy (Russ.) 1828-1910	
	Ibsen (Norw.) 1828-1906	Millais (Eng.) 1829-96
Brahms (Ger.) 1833-97	C. Rossetti (Eng.) 1830-94	Manet (Fr.) 1832-1883
Borodin (Russ.) 1834-87	William Morris (Eng.) 1834-96	Whistler (Amer.) 1834-1903
	W.S. Gilbert (Eng.) 1836-1911	Degas (Fr.) 1834-1917
Bizet (Fr.) 1838-75		
Mussorgsky (Russ.) 1839-81		Cézanne (Fr.) 1839-1906
Tchaikovsky (Russ.) 1840-93	Hardy (Eng.) 1840-1928	Rodin (Fr.) 1840-1917
	Zola (Fr.) 1840-1902	Monet (Fr.) 1840-1926
Dvořák (Czech) 1841-1904		Renoir (Fr.) 1841-1919
Sullivan (Eng.) 1842-1900	Mallarmé (Fr.) 1842-98	
Grieg (Norw.) 1843-1907	Henry James (Amer.) 1843-1916	
	Verlaine (Fr.) 1844-96	
	Bridges (Eng.) 1844-1930	
Fauré (Fr.) 1845-1924		
Parry (Eng.) 1848-1918	Strindberg (Swed.) 1849-1912	Gauguin (Fr.) 1849-1903
	R.L. Stevenson (Eng.) 1850-94	
Janáček (Czech) 1854-1928	Rimbaud (Fr.) 1854-91	Van Gogh (Fr.) 1853-90
Elgar (Eng.) 1857-1934	G.B. Shaw (Irish) 1856-1950	Louis Sullivan (Amer.)
		1856-1924
Puccini (It.) 1858-1924	Seurat (Fr.) 1859-91	
Wolf (Austr.) 1860-1903	Chekhov (Russ.) 1860-1904	
Mahler (Austr.) 1860-1911		
Debussy (Fr.) 1862-1918		
Delius (Eng.) 1862-1934	Gorky (Russ.) 1863-1936	Munch (Norw.) 1863-1944
R. Strauss (Ger.) 1864-1949		
Sibelius (Finn.) 1865-1957	Kipling (Eng.) 1865-1936	
Nielsen (Dan.) 1865-1931	Yeats (Irish) 1865-1939	
Satie (Fr.) 1866-1925	H.G. Wells (Eng.) 1866-1946	Kandinsky (Russ.) 1866-1944
	Galsworthy (Eng.) 1867-1933	Matisse (Fr.) 1869-1954
		Lloyd Wright (Amer.) 1869-1959

Compositions, books, plays, buildings and works of Art	Some other significant people and events
Beethoven's *Fidelio* (1st version) 1805 Goya's *Execution of the Defenders of Madrid* 1809	Isambard Kingdom Brunel 1806-59 Charles Darwin 1809-82
Jane Austen's *Pride and Prejudice* 1813 Constable's *Flatford Mill* 1817	Napoleon retreats from Moscow 1812 Philharmonic Society of London founded 1813 Battle of Waterloo 1815 Karl Marx 1818-83
Weber's *Der Freischütz*, Berlin 1821	Stockton and Darlington Railway 1821-5
Schubert's *Die schöne Müllerin* 1823 Beethoven's 9th Symphony 1825	
Berlioz's *Symphonie fantastique* 1829	
Turner's *Norham Castle* 1835-40 Dickens' *Pickwick Papers* 1836	Slavery prohibited in British colonies 1834
	Queen Victoria comes to the throne 1837
Houses of Parliament 1840-52	Penny post introduced 1840
	F.W. Nietzche 1844-1900
Mendelssohn's *Elijah* performed at Birmingham 1846 Millais' *Ophelia* 1852	Irish Potato Famine 1847 *Communist Manifesto* 1848 The Great Exhibition 1851
	Sigmund Freud 1856-1939
Darwin's *Origin of Species* 1859 Wagner's *Tristan und Isolde* 1859	
Hugo's *Les Misérables* 1862	Emancipation of Negroes 1863
Smetana's *Bartered Bride* 1866 Wagner's *Meistersinger* 1867 George Eliot writes *Middlemarch* 1870	

COMPARATIVE CHRONOLOGY

Composers	Poets and writers	Artists and architects
Vaughan Williams (Eng.) 1872-1958	Proust (Fr.) 1871-1922	Mondrian (Dutch) 1872-1944
Rakhmaninov (Russ.) 1873-1943	Synge (Irish) 1871-1909	
Holst (Eng.) 1874-1934	de la Mare (Eng.) 1873-1956	
Schoenberg (Austr.) 1874-1951		
Ives (Amer.) 1874–1954		
Ravel (Fr.) 1875-1937	Rilke (Austr.) 1875-1926	
	Mann (Ger.) 1875-1955	Brancusi (Roum.) 1876-1957
Ireland (Eng.) 1879-1962	Forster (Eng.) 1879-1972	Klee (Swiss) 1879-1940
		Marc (Ger.) 1880-1916
Bloch (Swiss) 1880-1959	Sean O'Casey (Irish) 1880-1964	Epstein (Eng.) 1880-1959
Bartók (Hung.) 1881-1945		Picasso (Sp.) 1881-1973
Kodály (Hung.) 1882-1967	Joyce (Irish) 1882-1941	Braque (Fr.) 1882-1963
Stravinsky (Russ.) 1882-1971		
Bax (Eng.) 1883-1953	Kafka (Czech) 1883-1924	Utrillo (Fr.) 1883-1955
Webern (Austr.) 1883-1945		Gropius (Ger.) 1883-1969
		Modigliani (It.) 1884-1920
Berg (Austr.) 1885-1935	D.H. Lawrence (Eng.) 1885-1930	Kokoschka (Austr.) 1886-
		L. S. Lowry (Eng.) 1887-1976
		Archipenko (Russ.) 1887-1964
		Arp (Fr.) 1887-1966
	T.S. Eliot (Eng.) 1888-1965	Paul Nash (Eng.) 1889-1946
	Cocteau (Fr.) 1889-1963	Chagall (Russ.) 1889-1985
Prokofiev (Russ.) 1891-1953		Spencer (Eng.) 1891-1959
Bliss (Eng.) 1891-1975		Ernst (Ger.) 1891-1976
		Luigi Nervi (It.) 1891-
	J.B. Priestley (Eng.) 1894-1984	Miró (Sp.) 1893-
Hindemith (Ger.) 1895-1963	Graves (Eng.) 1895-1985	
Orff (Ger.) 1895-1982		
	Scott Fitzgerald (Amer.) 1896-1940	Le Corbusier (Swiss) 1887-1965
Gershwin (Amer.) 1898-1937	Hemingway (Amer.) 1898-1961	Henry Moore (Eng.) 1898-1986
	Brecht (Ger.) 1898-1956	Calder (Amer.) 1898-1976
Poulenc (Fr.) 1899-1963		
Copland (Amer.) 1900-		
A. Bush (Eng.) 1900-		
Weill (Ger.) 1900-1950		
Rubbra (Eng.) 1901-86		Giacometti (Swiss) 1901-66
Walton (Eng.) 1902-1983	Steinbeck (Amer.) 1902-68	
Berkeley Lennox (Eng.) 1903-	Orwell (Eng.) 1903-50	Sutherland (Eng.) 1903-86
		Hepworth (Eng.) 1903-
		Rothko (Russ.) 1903-70
Kabalevsky (Russ.) 1904-87	Isherwood (Amer.) 1904-86	Salvador Dali (Sp.) 1904-
	Greene (Eng.) 1904-	

Compositions, books, plays, buildings and works of Art	Some other significant people and events
Verdi's *Aida* 1871	
	Sergey Diaghilev 1872-1929
First Impressionist Exhibition 1874 Mussorgsky's *Boris Godunov* 1874	
Bizet's *Carmen* 1875 Wagner's *Ring of the Nibelung* at Bayreuth 1876	
	Mikhail Fokine 1880-1942
Stevenson's *Treasure Island* 1883	
Mahler's Symphony No. 1 1888	
	Hitler 1889-1945
Tchaikovsky's *Sleeping Beauty* 1890	
Verdi's *Falstaff* 1893 Louis Sullivan's Guaranty Building at Buffalo 1895 Strauss's *Till Eulenspiegel* 1895 Hardy's *Jude the Obscure* 1896	Alexander Korda 1893-1956 Marconi invents wireless telegraphy 1895 Queen's Hall Promenade Concerts started 1895 English Folk Song Society founded 1898 Eisenstein 1898-1948
Schoenberg's *Verklärte Nacht* 1899 Elgar's *Dream of Gerontius* 1900	Freud's *Interpretation of Dreams* 1900
	Death of Queen Victoria 1901
Debussy's *Pelléas et Mélisande* 1902 Debussy's *La Mer* 1903-5 Shaw's *Man and Superman* 1903	
	George Balanchine 1904-83

COMPARATIVE CHRONOLOGY

Composers	Poets and writers	Artists and architects
Rawsthorne (Eng.) 1905-1971	C.P. Snow (Eng.) 1905-80	
Tippett (Eng.) 1905-	Sartre (Fr.) 1905-1980	
Shostakovitch (Russ.) 1906-1975	Betjeman (Eng.) 1906-1984	
Williams, Grace (Welsh) 1906-1977	Beckett (Irish) 1906-	
Lutyens (Eng.) 1906-83		
Maconchy (Eng.) 1907-	Auden (Eng.) 1907-1974	
	MacNeice (Irish) 1907-63	Pasmore (Eng.) 1908-
Messiaen (Fr.) 1908-		Vasarely (Hung.) 1908-
		Bacon (Eng.) 1909-
Menotti (It.) 1911-		
Cage (Amer.) 1912-	Ionesco (Roum.) 1912-	Pollock (Amer.) 1912-56
Jones, Daniel (Welsh) 1912-		
Britten (Eng.) 1913-76	Camus (Fr.) 1913-60	
Lutosławski (Polish) 1913-	Arthur Miller (Amer.) 1915-	
		Nolan (Australian) 1917-
Bernstein (Amer.) 1918-	Solzhenitsyn (Russ.) 1918-	
Hamilton (Scot.) 1922-	Larkin (Eng.) 1922-85	
Ligeti (Hung.) 1923-		
Nono (It.) 1924-		Caro (Eng.) 1924
Boulez (Fr.) 1925-		
Berio (It.) 1925-		
Henze (Ger.) 1926-		
Musgrave (Scot.) 1928-		
Hoddinott (Welsh) 1929-	Gunn (Eng.) 1929-	
	Osborne (Eng.) 1929-	
	Pinter (Eng.) 1930-	Warhol (Amer.) c.1930-87
	Hughes (Eng.) 1930-	
Williamson (Australian) 1931-		
	Wesker (Eng.) 1932-	
Penderecki (Polish) 1933-		
Birtwistle (Eng.) 1934-		
Maxwell Davies (Eng.) 1934-		
Mathias (Welsh) 1934-		
R.R. Bennett (Eng.) 1936-		Hockney (Eng.) 1937-

Compositions, books, plays, buildings and works of Art	Some other significant people and events
	Einstein's Theory of Relativity 1905
Galsworthy's *Man of Property* 1906	
Synge's *Playboy of the Western World* 1907	
Mahler's *Symphony of a Thousand* (No. 8) Munich 1910 Ravel's *Daphnis et Chloé* 1911 Schoenberg's *Pierrot Lunaire* 1912	
Stravinsky's *Rite of Spring* 1913 D.H. Lawrence's *Sons and Lovers* 1913	First World War 1914-1918 Russian Revolution 1917
Holst's *Planets* performed 1918 Joyce's *Ulysses* 1922 Kafka's *The Trial* 1925 Gropius' Bauhaus built 1925-6 Berg's *Wozzeck* 1926	Alcock and Brown fly across Atlantic 1919 Einsenstein's film *The Battleship Potemkin* 1925
	Wall Street crash 1929
Stravinsky's *Symphony of Psalms* 1930 Luigi's Stadium, Florence 1930-2 Walton's *Belshazzar's Feast* 1931 Vaughan Williams' *Job* 1931	
	Korda's film *The Private Life of Henry VIII* 1932 Hitler became Chancellor of Germany 1933
Bartók's *Music for Strings, Percussion and celeste* 1936 Picasso's *Guernica* 1937	Spanish Civil War 1936